A World of Her Own

24 Amazing Women Explorers and Adventurers

MICHAEL ELSOHN ROSS

CHICAGO
REVIEW
PRESS

Copyright © 2014 by Michael Elsohn Ross
All rights reserved
Published by Chicago Review Press, Incorporated
814 North Franklin Street
Chicago, Illinois 60610

ISBN 978-1-61374-438-3

Cover and interior design: Sarah Olson

Library of Congress Cataloging-in-Publication Data

Ross, Michael Elsohn, 1952-
  A world of her own : 24 amazing women explorers and adventurers / Michael
Elsohn Ross.
     pages cm — (Women of action)
  Includes bibliographical references and index.
  ISBN 978-1-61374-438-3 (hardback)
  1. Women explorers—Biography. I. Title.

  G200.R66 2014
  910.92'5—dc23

                              2013024947

Printed in the United States of America
5 4 3 2 1

This book is dedicated to my remarkable grandnieces; the young women of my village, El Portal; and youthful readers everywhere. May these stories ignite a desire to take a step beyond the known.

You have legs, you can go;
You have a voice, why not sing?
You have a heart, dance!
—Nanao Sakaki, *Break the Mirror*

Contents

— — — — —

PART IV: LONG TREKS

Introduction

WOMEN WITH WANDERLUST

Picture joining a potluck birthday party attended by 24 women, each one bringing tales of her wild adventures along with exotic foods from places she has explored. Everyone is celebrating Jill and Stephanie's birthdays. Both were born on January 1. As you wander through the crowd, you listen in on one conversation after another. At the edge of the field, Jill and Helen take bites of smoked salmon and gesticulate dramatically as they discuss voracious bears they have encountered. Nearby on a small hill, Constanza, Annie, Sophia, and Rosaly eat Andean potatoes while talking of the high mountains they have climbed. Lounging on a picnic blanket chewing venison jerky, Martha and Isabella compare adventures in the Rocky Mountains, and a short distance away, Aparajita and Ynes snack on roasted grubs, laughing about encounters with tropical leeches and giant cockroaches. Stephanie and Edie, between bites of sushi, describe their first underwater experiences. Not far from them, Pamela and Lorie dine on dal and rice as they chat about bird discoveries. Under a large tree, Helga and Alexandra sample *tsampa* and oatmeal as they swap stories of their long treks. Above them, perched on a stout limb, Kate and Margaret munch on mangoes and compare encounters with venomous snakes. Out by the pond, Kay and Eleanor drink grog and soak their bare feet in the cool water, exchanging tales of their sea voyages. Seated on a tree stump, Freya and Kira nibble on olives and chuckle about their experiences evading authorities intent on restricting their travels. Watching it all is Marianne, who paints the scene before her and smiles at the sight of Annie weaving in and out of the crowd on her bicycle.

This scene can only be imagined, because some of the women you will meet in this book lived long before others were even born. As you get to know each woman, I invite you to revisit this imaginary potluck picnic, as well as picture yourself as one of the next generation of women explorers and adventurers.

Lorie Karnath

A PRESIDENT OF EXPLORERS

> *"When I first landed in Antarctica, I got out of the airplane and immediately I was frozen cold, but before I even realized that, what I saw was the most amazing sight: Everything looked like glittering diamonds—from the air to the hills to the ice below me—it was just sparkling and so awe-inspiring that I knew in that second, this is why I do it."*
>
> —*Lorie Karnath*

The first explorers to reach the North Pole, the South Pole, the world's highest peak, and the surface of the Moon all were men. Each of them also belonged to the Explorers Club, which for its first 77 years was an all-male club, headquartered in New York City. The club functioned as a gathering place for explorers to share their discoveries and talk shop. It also served as a repository for artifacts and journals from members' expeditions.

Exceptional women explorers had been making remarkable discoveries during the preceding centuries, but it wasn't until the 1980s that they were invited to become members of the club.

And it wasn't until the year 2000 that the Explorers Club finally elected Faanya L. Rose as its first woman president. In 2009, explorer Lorie Karnath became the second woman to lead the club. She took on the mission of actively honoring the club's history while at the same time redefining the image of explorers.

In the early 1960s in Concord, Massachusetts, Lorie and her brothers frequently investigated the nearby woods. They captured snakes, frogs, grasshoppers, and other critters and brought them home to observe but not keep as pets. All of the animals were released back into the wild. Lorie's parents, Albert and Carole, shared their children's interest in nature and actively encouraged these backyard explorations. Lorie said that starting early in her life, her parents showed her and her siblings many amazing things the planet has to offer. They encouraged their children to learn through experience.

More than 100 years earlier, the famous naturalist Henry David Thoreau had lived nearby at Walden Pond. The Karnath

Lorie Karnath in Bhutan with rice paddies across the river.
Courtesy of Lorie Karnath

Lorie Karnath holds the Wings WorldQuest Flag #14 at Ruehstaedt, Germany. The signs show the distances to nearby stork colonies and migration destinations.
Courtesy of Lorie Karnath

family took walks there, and Lorie learned about Thoreau's friends Ralph Waldo Emerson and also Louisa May Alcott, who became one of her heroes. At the age of 10, Lorie moved to Europe with her family, where they continued to explore. As they traveled around Europe, Lorie came to recognize the differences between well-trod tourist spots, the more genuine communities, and lesser-known historic sites where few tourists ventured.

As an adult, Lorie continued to have a passion for asking questions and following the answers wherever they led her. In 2007 she traveled through Europe and Africa tracking migrating white storks; she observed their nests, examined threats, and established a wetlands reserve. On walks in the woods surrounding her home in the Hudson River valley in New York, Lorie has spent hours watching bald eagles, fox, deer, and other wildlife, and each day she has asked new questions. Whether exploring in Antarctica, Africa, Asia, or South America, she always has brought home questions. Lorie has endured harsh field conditions, such as leech-infested jungles, scorching heat, and heavy rains while studying flora and fauna in Borneo. Her skill on horseback proved indispensable on her ride across the

Tibetan Plateau, the world's highest and largest plateau which includes Tibet, as well as sections of China and India.

As president of the Explorers Club, Lorie's job was to support explorers—experienced ones, such as Brazilian volcanologist Rosaly Lopes, and newcomers, such as Sewa Tripathi, a student of botany in Nepal. Lorie's work for the club kept her from exploring as much as she would have liked, but as president she had the chance to promote exploration as a vital process in learning about our world and how to sustain it. Whether on a stroll in New York City or on a climb up an Alpine peak, Lorie has always carried the spirit of exploration with her. When she faces challenges at work or home, she relies on the skills of endurance and flexibility that all explorers develop. Most of all, she always holds in her mind memories of journeys and the children in remote places for whose education she has raised funds.

On one of the walls of the Explorers Club headquarters in New York City is a photograph of mountaineer Annie Smith Peck. Annie is one of the many explorers Lorie admires and one of the women you will discover in this book.

"I have five words that I think our activity at the Explorers Club revolves around: explore, discover, share, preserve, and sustain," Lori stated on the *National Geographic* blog. "So basically go out and discover, share our knowledge, give back to the community and government, work with businesses and bench scientists, and tell what we have seen out there. . . . Explorers today figure out ways to preserve and sustain the things that are critical in our lives. Exploration must be focused on learning and bringing back—and adding to our overall body of knowledge."

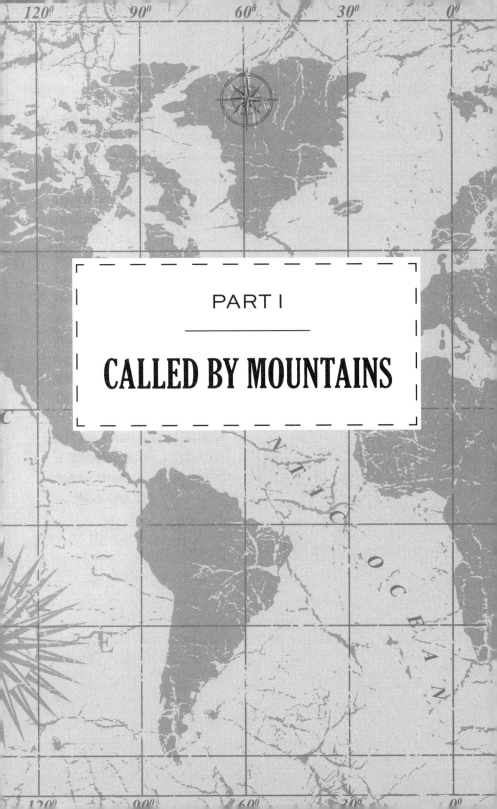

PART I

CALLED BY MOUNTAINS

Annie Smith Peck

A WOMAN ABOVE THEM ALL

"Men, we all know, climb in knickerbockers. Women, on the contrary, will declare that a skirt is no hindrance to their loco-motion. This is obviously absurd. . . . For a woman in difficult mountaineering to waste her strength and endanger her life with a skirt is foolish in the extreme." —Annie Smith Peck

On her sixth attempt to achieve the first ascent of Huascarán, the highest mountain in Peru, Annie Smith Peck and her climbing party endured howling wind, ice-crusted snow, and subzero temperatures. As the team crossed an ice bridge across a glacial crevasse, one of the porters slipped and fell. Fortunately, he was roped to the other climbers, who hauled him out uninjured. Unfortunately, his pack remained deep in the bottom of the crevasse. In it was a gas stove needed to melt snow for drinking water. Without drinking water they would have to turn back. However, they were able to continue after Gabriel, one of the Swiss mountain guides, fearlessly descended into the crevasse and retrieved the pack. It wasn't until late in the afternoon of the following day, August 31, 1908, that they reached the summit. Standing at the 21,833-foot peak, Annie Smith Peck had finally climbed higher than any other woman mountaineer in the Americas. As the group started the journey back down the mountain, Annie wondered if they would survive the perilous descent.

Born on October 19, 1850, in Providence, Rhode Island, Annie grew up far away from any peaks. The highest elevation in her home state was just a little more than 800 feet. Both her mother and father were from families that had settled in Rhode Island more than 200 years before Annie's birth. Her father was a prosperous lawyer and politician.

With three rambunctious older brothers, Annie naturally developed a tough and competitive character. She was just as bright as her brothers, but during this era women had few career options besides teaching. Thus Annie chose to earn a teaching certificate at Rhode Island Normal School (now Rhode Island College), though being in the classroom was not her ultimate goal. After teaching high school students for a short time, she decided to continue her education. She wanted to attend Brown University in Providence as her father and brothers had, but she was refused admission due to her gender.

Undeterred, Annie applied to the University of Michigan and was accepted as one of its first female students. After earning her bachelor's degree, she took time off to teach at a high school before returning to the university. In 1881 she was awarded a master's degree, specializing in Greek. That same year, she was appointed as a professor at Purdue University in West Lafayette, Indiana, to teach Latin, elocution, and German—one of the first women college professors in the nation.

Despite this achievement, Annie was determined to continue her studies as her brothers had. She saved up enough money to travel to Germany to study music and improve her

German. After a year she moved to Greece, where she became the first woman to enroll at the American School of Classical Studies in Athens. It was in Greece that she climbed her first two mountains. Before returning home, Annie visited Switzerland and saw the Alps, including the towering Matterhorn Peak, for the first time. It was a life-changing experience.

Annie later wrote, "My allegiance, previously given to the sea, was transferred for all time to the mountains, the Matterhorn securing the first place in my affections."

From that moment Annie wanted to climb mountains, despite having learned that many climbers died ascending the Matterhorn, including members of the team that first reached its summit in 1865. She learned it had been summited in 1871 by Lucy Walker—an Englishwoman who climbed wearing a white print dress—and later that year by Meta Brevoort—an American who reached the summit garbed in men's pants.

Back home, Annie's growing reputation as a scholar led to an offer to teach at Smith College in Northampton, Massachusetts, but at this point she was hooked by the romance of adventure. Though Annie was happy, her conservative parents were upset by her independent nature and desire for further education. After they learned of their daughter's plans to become a mountain climber, they practically disowned her. These concerns did not deter Annie from pursuing her dreams.

In 1888, Annie and her brother George scrambled up Clouds Rest, a massive granite peak in California's Sierra Nevada range (now part of Yosemite National Park). Annie felt exhilarated by climbing, especially as she loped up Mount Shasta, a 14,162-foot-high volcano in Northern California. In 1895, wearing a hip-length woolen tunic, a wide-brimmed hat, baggy-kneed trousers normally worn by boys, and calf-length canvas puttees, Annie ascended the Matterhorn, becoming the third woman to stand atop the famous peak. Both her mountaineering feat and her climbing costume earned Annie notoriety. During that period in America, in places such as Arkansas, women were being arrested for wearing bloomers (long, baggy pants). Annie's courage and audacity struck a chord with American women, who were seeking the right to vote, more social freedoms, and professional opportunities. The Singer Sewing Company gave away a photograph of Annie dressed in her climbing outfit with every sewing machine sold. This fame enabled Annie to earn her living by lecturing. On a placard that advertised her appearances, she proclaimed herself the "Queen of Climbing." Most women back then considered themselves old at the age of 45, but not Annie. She was poised to accomplish even more spectacular climbs of loftier peaks.

With payment she received from the *New York World* to write a newspaper story, Annie organized an expedition to the summits of Popocatepetl and Orizaba in Mexico. Despite these two volcanoes being much higher than the Matterhorn, ascending them was a less dangerous affair:

Annie Smith Peck in her daring mountaineering outfit.
Library of Congress

neither required technical climbing on rock face. In 1897, when Annie reached the summit of Orizaba, the third highest peak in North America, she broke the record for the highest elevation yet attained by a female climber. When the ascent of Popocatepetl didn't match the "death defying" feat promoted by the newspaper, Annie's article described her climb as more dangerous than it actually was.

"My next thought was to do a little genuine exploration to conquer a virgin peak, to attain some height where no man had previously stood," Annie later wrote of her ambitions at this point in her life. She set her sights on South America, picking Sorata in Bolivia—thought at the time to be the highest peak on that continent. It took four long years for Annie to raise enough funds for the expedition, but finally on June 16, 1903, she boarded a ship bound for South America as the leader of her expedition. Traveling with her was a team of two experienced Swiss mountain guides and a professor of geology. The expedition's gear included compasses, four cameras, oxygen tanks, a camp stove, and rifles and handguns, as well as Admiral Robert E. Peary's Inuit suit, which he had brought back from the Arctic. The *New York Times* stated that Mount Sorata was estimated to be anywhere from 21,500 to 24,800 feet high. (It is now called Mount Illampu and is actually 20,892 feet high.)

Annie felt well prepared to reach the summit, but she was thwarted by the men in her expedition who turned back after reaching an elevation of more than 15,000 feet. The professor suffered from altitude sickness, and the sandal-clad porters understandably refused to trek through the deep snow. Annie was bitterly disappointed at having to turn back.

Annie's next choice was another high Peruvian peak, Huascarán, thought to be between 23,000 and 24,000 feet high. To get to this remote mountain region 450 miles south of Lima,

Annie had to travel via train, boat, and finally on horseback to the town of Yungay. From there, at the foot of the mountain, she gazed upward in awe.

"The immense glacier below the peaks was so visibly and terribly cut by a multitude of crevasses that it seemed impossible for the most skillful, much less for men wholly inexperienced, to find a way through such a maze," Annie wrote of her coming challenge.

Locals doubted that the summit could be reached. Annie disregarded these apprehensions and departed on September 28, 1904, accompanied by a procession of well-wishers, including the governor and a local newspaper editor. Also along with her was an American man named Peter, whom she had hired to assist on the climb. By the fourth day of their ascent, they came within reach of the saddle between the twin peaks. Avalanches that cascaded down through the saddle forced them to

The massive Huascarán.
Courtesy of Maurice Chédel / Wikimedia Commons

switch to a more difficult route over rocky terrain. This ascent became worse when they were caught in a blizzard. Annie was determined to continue, but Peter refused to carry her climbing irons and camera, and the porters were unwilling to advance. Once again Annie was forced to retreat. But only five days after returning to Yungay, she set off again with five stalwart indigenous porters. As they neared the route to the saddle, their progress was slowed by a hazardous maze of crevasses and another blizzard. The several days needed to reach the summit required extensive climbing on ice and snow. Annie feared that her porters, who lacked warm clothing, would not survive the harsh conditions, so she turned back, vowing to make another attempt.

In less than two years Annie returned. This time she had funding from *Harper's* magazine in exchange for an article about her adventure. Both this climb and the next one were thwarted when porters refused to continue on to higher, more dangerous elevations, but Annie refused to give up. In August 1908 Annie returned to Yungay accompanied by two Swiss guides. On their first attempt, one of the guides, Rudolf, suffered from altitude sickness, and the other, more dependable guide, Gabriel, exhausted himself trying to do double duty. With just the one guide and two porters, Annie ascended to her highest point yet, the saddle between Huascarán's twin peaks. Though they were within reach of the summit, it was too late in the day to press on. Gabriel was totally exhausted and their food supplies were nearly gone, so Annie decided to retreat.

Finally, at the end of August, Annie and her party set off once more. It was her sixth attempt, and she was more determined than ever to succeed. Though the final section of the climb below the summit was particularly treacherous, they climbed with extreme care and reached the summit in the late afternoon.

Annie was elated but worried. She knew that descending in the dark would be particularly hazardous and that they must start back soon. She lingered to take photos from atop the peak but, anxious to make use of the remaining daylight, decided not to take time to measure the elevation.

Annie remembered the descent as "a horrible nightmare." During the 48 hours it took to get off the mountain, they went without food or water. Annie slipped multiple times but was securely roped to Gabriel, who held on tight. Meanwhile, Rudolf, the other guide, lost his gloves, and his hands became badly frozen. As soon as they reached Yungay, they rushed him to a doctor. The damage was so severe that the doctor had to amputate one hand, a finger from his other hand, and half of one foot to prevent his death from gangrene.

News of her triumphant ascent was cabled around the world. Annie, who was then almost 60 years old, was a greater celebrity than ever. But her overestimation of the true elevation of

the peak caused a controversy. Her claim to have reached an elevation of 24,000 feet, a world record for any climber, man or woman, rankled another

This trading card that pictures Annie Smith Peck came free with a pack of cigarettes.
Russell A. Potter Collection

MISS ANNIE S. PECK

woman mountaineer, Fanny Bullock Workman, who had reached an elevation of 23,300 feet in the Himalayas. Fanny and her husband paid to have the height of Huascarán measured, and it was determined to be only 21,811 feet high. Annie was not happy with the news and later responded in her first book, "$13,000 seems a large sum to spend for the triangulation of a single mountain which it cost but $3,000 to climb. With $1,000 more for my expedition, I should have been able with an assistant to triangulate the peak myself."

For the next few years, Annie divided her time between writing a book about her climbing adventures in South America and attending rallies demanding voting rights for women. In 1911, when Annie ascended Nevado Coropuna, Peru's second highest peak, she planted a banner emblazoned with VOTES FOR WOMEN on the summit. Later that same year, her book *Search for the Apex of America: High Mountain Climbing in Peru and Bolivia Including the Conquest of Huascarán, with Some Observations on the Country and People Below* was published.

Unlike other women explorers who came from prosperous families, Annie financed her bare-bones expeditions without her parents' help. As a woman expedition leader, she experienced additional hardships not endured by male leaders. The men on her climbing teams often ignored her suggestions and attempted to take advantage of her financially, but they soon became aware, as her friend Amelia Earhart stated, that "Miss Peck would make almost anyone appear soft." Annie Smith Peck made her mark as an independent and determined adventurer and entertaining author.

In 1928, when Annie was 78 years old, the northern peak of the Huascarán was named *Cumbre Aña Peck* in her honor. In 1929 she embarked on two years of air travel around South America, covering 20,000 miles, and at the age of 80 she wrote her fourth and final book about her travels in South America. A short time later, she climbed to the top of New Hampshire's Mount Madison. It was her last climb. In 1935 Annie had to cancel a 75-day world tour when her health deteriorated. She was nearly 85 years old and had seen the country change to one where women could not only wear pants to climb a mountain, but they could vote as well. After returning to Manhattan, Annie died at home on July 18.

Rosaly Lopes

WHERE PASSION LEADS

> *"I was always adventurous, and I thought seeing a volcano erupt sounded more interesting than going to some cold observatory somewhere." —Dr. Rosaly Lopes*

In 1981 Italy's Mount Etna erupted explosively, spurting up jets of molten rock 600 feet into the sky. Within a period of six hours, lava had flowed two miles down the mountainside, covering acres of farmland. Fortunately, only a few homes were destroyed; most of the lava had flowed between the two villages below the mountaintop. As soon as news of the eruption reached London University, Rosaly Lopes and her professor, Dr. John Guest, along with the other scientists on the UK Volcanic Eruption Surveillance Team madly rushed to catch a flight to Sicily, Italy. Due to delays they arrived at Mount Etna after the eruption had apparently ceased.

As Rosaly and John walked up the volcano to investigate a new 50-foot-high cone, a sound like broken glass fragments rubbing against one another alerted them that lava was still moving. Just as John said, "This thing is not dead yet," the cone exploded,

A print from 1840 shows the eruption of Mount Etna.
Courtesy of Wikimedia Commons

sending fiery lava bombs into the air. Rosaly peered above her, ready to dodge any falling lava that might come their way. John had instructed his students never to run, because it is safer to keep an eye on the falling fragments of glowing rock. She was thus surprised when he shouted, "Run!" Together they dashed downhill to safety. With his years of experience of being around erupting volcanoes, John had judged that the bombs hadn't shot out very far from the cone. Therefore he and Rosaly could get out of their range before they hit.

Three years before, in 1979, Rosaly was 22 when she witnessed her first eruption, on this very same mountain. That July the southeast crater exploded and shot red-hot fragments more than 300 feet high. Later in September, Rosaly, John, and other members of the volcano surveillance team were about a mile away from the crater when they felt a ground tremor. Suddenly, a black cloud of ash spewed from the top of the crater.

As on most summer days, there was a crowd of tourists at the top. During the eruption there was total chaos while the crowd of about 150 people ran about, desperately dodging the falling lava bombs. Nine people were killed, including both parents of a young boy as well as a newlywed on his honeymoon. Many others were injured. Rosaly joined her team in caring for injured survivors, and she never forgot the anguish of those who saw their loved ones die. At this point Rosaly took on the mission to better understand volcanic eruptions in hopes of preventing future disasters.

"In one evening, Etna taught me that the work of a volcanologist is not all science and adventure. Our science had failed these people, because we still know so little about how volcanoes work," Rosaly recounts in her book *The Volcano Adventure Guide*.

Rosaly Lopes was born on January 8, 1957, in Rio de Janeiro, Brazil. As a young child it was space travel, not volcanoes, that was on her mind. At the age of four, her parents told her that a Russian man had gone into space. She had no clue what a Russian was, and her only notion of space was "somewhere way up in the sky." But when her father asked her if she wanted to go into space when she grew up, she enthusiastically answered yes. The idea became lodged in her brain, and as she grew older she

A future space explorer at age four.
Courtesy of Rosaly Lopes

shared this desire with adults who asked what she wanted to do when she grew up. Most of them thought it was a cute ambition and humored her, assuming she would soon forget about it.

In reality, Rosaly's wish to explore space as an astronaut only grew stronger. In school she earned excellent grades and started studying French and English with private teachers. Though Brazil did have a small space program, it had no astronauts. Even at NASA, the US space program, there had not yet been any women astronauts. Eventually it dawned on Rosaly that her poor eyesight and gender might prevent her from achieving her goal, and she decided to become an astronomer instead.

In 1970, when she was 13 years old, Rosaly read a news report about the mechanical failures on the Apollo 13 mission spacecraft that had prevented it from landing on the moon and almost left the astronauts stranded in space. What caught her eye was the story of how the astronauts were brought safely home due to the calculations of a young woman mathematician at NASA's mission control center. She was the only one able to plot the spacecraft's course back to Earth. In the paper was a photo of the pretty, young blond computer specialist named Poppy Northcutt. Rosaly was astounded and encouraged. From that point on, her goal was to be a NASA astronomer. Concerned that her daughter's plan might not be achievable, Mrs. Lopes suggested that Rosaly take typing so she could be a secretary if her plans didn't work out. Rosaly rejected this suggestion as unnecessary. And indeed her acceptance into the astronomy program at the University of London set her on a course to eventually work with NASA. With her parents' total support Rosaly took off across the sea for Great Britain, where her French would be of little use.

It wasn't until in 1978, when she was in Dr. John Guest's planetary geology class, that Rosaly developed her interest in volcanoes. One day Professor Guest didn't show up for class, and his substitute explained that Dr. Guest had gone to observe Mount Etna's latest eruption. Rosaly was intrigued. After graduating with her degree in astronomy, she asked Dr. Guest if she could be one of his graduate students. Despite the fact that she would be the only one of his students without a geology degree, he gladly accepted her.

"He told me I couldn't understand volcanoes on other planets if I didn't understand them on Earth," Rosaly remembered years later.

From that point on, all it took to get her hooked was for Rosaly to witness her first eruption of Mount Etna in 1979. Then she could combine her new fascination for volcanoes and her lifelong passion with outer space. During the next eight years she observed and compared eruptions on Earth with those on Mars. Her studies included Olympus Mons, the largest volcano in the solar system. This immense volcano on Mars covers an area about the size of Arizona and is three times as tall as Mount Everest, Earth's highest peak.

After she earned her doctorate degree in planetary science, Rosaly worked for the next three and a half years at the Royal Observatory in Greenwich, Great Britain, one of the world's oldest and most important scientific centers. She continued her studies of volcanic activity on both Earth and Mars. In 1989 she went to Italy to conduct research at Osservatorio Vesuviano in Naples, near the famous volcano Mount Vesuvius.

Her next move was in 1996 to the Jet Propulsion Laboratory (JPL) in Southern California, where she finally fulfilled her childhood dream of working with NASA. Her work, however, was not in support of manned space missions as she had once imagined. Rosaly arrived just in time to be involved with the Galileo Flight Project. This mission used two spacecraft—an orbiter and an

Rosaly Lopes, the world's record holder for most volcanoes discovered, kneels at the rim of Mount Yasur in Vanuatu.
Ralph White

atmospheric probe—that enabled scientists to collect information: at first about Venus and asteroids and eventually Jupiter and its moon Io. Using the near infrared spectrometer, she and fellow team members monitored Jupiter and Io for the next five years. Rosaly explored the surface of Io from 365 million miles away using data sent back from the probe. She skillfully detected 71 active volcanoes and is listed in the 2006 *Guinness World Records* book as the discoverer of the most volcanoes anywhere.

During these years, Rosaly also visited and studied volcanoes on her own planet. Her studies of volcanic activity on Io revealed that lava lakes are common there, but these pools of molten lava found in craters are quite rare on Earth. To understand Earth's lava lakes better, Rosaly traveled to the lava lake at Kilauea Volcano on the big island of Hawaii to examine it up close, and she planned to explore the other active lava lakes on Earth.

In 1996 during a filming project with Icelandic volcanologist Haraldur Sigurðsson on the Caribbean Island of Montserrat, Rosaly had a scare. While the camera was rolling, Haraldur had his back to an erupting volcano named English's Crater.

Unlike the slower flowing lava from Hawaiian volcanoes, the pyroclastic lava that flows from volcanoes like English's Crater can move at speeds of more than 100 mph. As Rosaly watched, the lava started pouring out faster and faster. She became so alarmed that she madly motioned to Haraldur to turn around, but he wasn't worried. With his extensive experience with pyroclastic eruptions on Iceland, he knew he was safe. However, early the next year English's Crater filled with lava, and by May some flowed over the rim. On June 25, 1997, 280 million cubic feet of molten rock broke loose and within 20 minutes killed 19 people. Subsequent eruptions eventually destroyed Plymouth, the island's capital. Fortunately, citizens had evacuated the city. Afterward, more than one half of the island was declared too dangerous to occupy.

Rosaly next investigated and photographed volcanoes in Hawaii, Mexico, Greece, Iceland, Costa Rica, and numerous areas in the United States. She also collected information about the human and geologic history of each site. On every visit she found herself answering questions for other visitors, and slowly an idea for a book evolved; she titled it *The Volcano Adventure Guide*. While completing the book, Rosaly joined the team of another NASA mission. The Cassini-Huygens spacecraft was launched in 1997 and reached Saturn in 2004. After orbiting the planet for six months, the Huygens probe was released from the Cassini orbiter. When it landed on Saturn, it became the first craft to ever alight in the outer solar system. At the Jet Propulsion Laboratory, Rosaly became coleader of an international team studying Titan, Saturn's biggest moon. Using data from the probe, she and her team discovered that Titan also has volcanic features. Unlike those on Earth or Io it appeared Titan's volcanoes are the result of ice volcanism. These ice volcanoes, technically called cryovolcanoes, were first detected in 1989 on Neptune's moon Triton by the *Voyager 2* spacecraft. Rosaly continued to investigate these far away volcanoes that spew ice, methane, and ammonia.

Since her volcano guide was published in 2005, Rosaly has explored more volcanoes while on her vacations or on side trips during conferences or speaking tours around the world. She has visited more than 50 countries on six of Earth's seven continents.

In 2011 she led an expedition in the Danakil Depression of Ethiopia to a place that was at the top of her wish list: the lava lake at the Erta Ale volcano.

"The lake appears to be alive, breathing and heaving, with exploding fire fountains. It was like being at the edge of Hell. I loved it!" wrote Rosaly after her visit.

Rosaly enjoying an erupting volcano in Vanuatu.
Bruce Williams

What alarmed Rosaly the most when visiting this lava lake was not any threat from volcanic eruptions but hearing gunshots while being escorted by Afar tribesmen equipped with AK-47s. She feared her group was under attack until she found out that the ruckus was actually from Australian tourists who had fired off their guides' guns just for fun.

It is hard to imagine that Rosaly finds time to meet with young people and talk about her passion for studying volcanoes, but during her many years of research and travel she has willingly given talks and appeared in numerous documentaries and TV shows. Her enthusiasm for inspiring students and informing the public resulted in her receiving the Carl Sagan Medal. Rosaly encourages young people, especially young women, to follow their interests and passions like she did. In her guidebook she writes, "I think that anyone, no matter what they do, should try to experience a volcanic eruption at least once in their life. This is why I wrote *The Volcano Adventure Guide*."

With her eyes on faraway moons and her feet climbing Earth's volcanoes, Dr. Rosaly Lopes continues her exploration of the explosive forces in our solar system.

Constanza Ceruti

CLIMBING SACRED MOUNTAINS
WITH A HUMBLE HEART

> *"When I was about 14, I climbed a hill and was entranced with seeing the horizons. Something special happened to me at that moment, and I dreamed about going to the mountains." —Constanza Ceruti*

It took five grueling days for Constanza Ceruti and other members of the archeology research team to haul supplies from their base camp at 16,000 feet on Mount Llullaillaco, in the Argentinian Andes, to a higher camp where they would be able to acclimatize to the thin air. This was a critical step in avoiding altitude sickness or, worse yet, a condition called pulmonary edema in which fluid builds up in the lungs. Despite this precaution, one of the team experienced this condition and was taken as quickly as possible to a lower elevation, where he received medical care. After setting up the main camp at 19,200 feet, Constanza and her coworkers attempted to reach the 22,110-foot-high mountaintop but were halted by 70 mph winds, subzero temperatures, and blowing snow. Their only recourse was to huddle inside their tents for the next four days, 200 feet below the summit, until conditions improved and they could continue upward to begin excavating at the top. When there, within a day and a half, Arcadio, one of the assistants, and his brother Ignacio unearthed a platform of stone and gravel. Five feet down was a well-preserved mummy. This was the highest elevation at which a mummy had ever been found. This was truly an unforgettable experience for Constanza, the 28-year-old coleader of the expedition, who was at the beginning of her career as an archaeologist.

Constanza Ceruti was born in Buenos Aires, Argentina's largest city, in 1973. Both of her parents were doctors. When she was a child they took her to museums, libraries, and city parks but never on walks in the countryside. She was fascinated by the variety of ancient artifacts she saw in museums and pored through the books about ancient history and cultures she found in her parents' large library. It was no wonder Constanza absorbed their interest in the stories and objects of ancient peoples.

One day when she was a teenager, Constanza joined friends on a hike up a hill outside the city. Here she got her first glimpse of the towering Andes, more than 100 miles away. It was a magical sight that left her with a great desire to explore the mountains. Later, after Constanza read an article about an archaeologist who had discovered artifacts high in the Andean peaks, she decided that was something she would like to do. However, her wish to visit the Andes took until 1995 to be fulfilled. By then she was nearly finished with her undergraduate studies in anthropology at the University of Buenos Aires and more than ready to climb her first high Andean peak.

"I felt completely whole and fulfilled and at peace in the mountains," Constanza later wrote.

Constanza Ceruti in Patagonia.
Courtesy of Constanza Ceruti

After her first trek in the high mountains of Patagonia, Constanza devoted her life to exploring high places. She climbed one mountain after another. After perfecting her mountaineering skills, she ascended Mount Aconcagua. At 22,841 feet it is the highest peak in the Americas as well as the tallest mountain in the Southern Hemisphere. Next, Constanza summited Mount Pissis, the Earth's second highest volcano, becoming the first woman to do so. Unlike many mountaineers who climb primarily to reach the summit, Constanza climbs in search of signs of past cultures, which she looks for on the mountainsides as well as at the summits. As Constanza learned about how indigenous mountain cultures revere high places, she strove to climb reverently. For Constanza, climbing became as much a spiritual experience as it was a physical and scientific exercise.

"Few mountain climbers will be happy to spend a month at the top after reaching the summit. On the other hand, most archaeologists will not enjoy the harsh climbing conditions. You have to like both mountaineering and archaeology very much to commit to this work," Constanza Ceruti wrote about the unique nature of her career.

Around the time that Constanza summited her first peak in 1995, an American archaeologist, Johan Reinhard, and his climbing partner, Miguel Zárate, discovered the frozen mummy of an Incan girl in the crater of the 20,630-foot-high Mount Amapo in southern Peru. At the time it was the best-preserved frozen human body yet discovered. Johan concluded that this mummy, later known as the "Ice Maiden," had been sacrificed to Incan gods and then buried more than 500 years ago. This ritual burial, known as capacocha, was practiced throughout the Incan Empire as an offering to the gods. Children were typically sacrificed because they were considered to be more pure than adults and were therefore a more powerful offering.

After graduating in 1996 with a degree in anthropology, Constanza began her doctoral studies at the University of Cuyo in Mendoza, Argentina. Now she was only a few hours away from the high Andes, and she started climbing peak after peak searching for archaeological sites. Before long she had a reputation as an ambitious and promising young archaeologist. In 1999, at the young age of 26, Constanza was chosen as codirector of four archaeological expeditions in the Andes with veteran archaeologist Johan Reinhard. Together they assembled a team that would carry out the physically demanding task of excavating archaeological sites at lofty elevations where oxygen levels are low and temperatures dip to $-30°$F.

In the winter of 1999 Constanza, Johan, and their team reached the summit of the 20,112-foot-high Nevado Quehuar in northern Argentina and were horrified to discover the mangled remains of a mummified child. The grave had been blasted open with dynamite by treasure hunters, and many of the ancient objects inside had been stolen. The mummy, preserved for so long in its grave, was left in pieces on the mountaintop. The team carefully salvaged the mummy's remains and collected the few ceremonial objects left behind. Any doubts Constanza had about removing these ancient artifacts from mountain-top tombs were erased by the acts of those grave robbers. She knew that, unlike treasure seekers, when she and her colleagues brought back human remains and ancient artifacts to museums, those items would be protected for others to view and study.

Less than two weeks later the team ascended the nearby peak, Llullaillaco (Yu-yai-YA-ko), for an extensive survey. On their way up they explored ancient Inca way stations located on a gentler route up the mountain than the one taken by current climbers.

"Just think of the Incas who made these ascents 400 years before the advent of modern mountaineering. They looked for the slope offering the easiest route up. That still makes sense today and improves my chance of encountering traces of their presence," wrote Constanza.

At the summit the team first discovered the mummy of a young boy. "The boy was wearing a typical male poncho. He had feathers on his forehead and a bracelet," Constanza wrote in her report. During the next 13 days of hard work the team uncovered two more frozen mummies, both of them girls.

"It is so humbling to look into the eyes of another human being from half a millennium ago," Constanza stated in her account of the experience.

Up until this point the Ice Maiden was the only well-preserved Incan mummy. Now they had found three more, even better

Constanza cleaning one of the mummies on Mount Llullaillaco.
Courtesy of Constanza Ceruti

preserved, frozen bodies of sacrificed children. Also uncovered were 20 clothed statues, as well as miniature figures of llamas made of gold, silver, and a type of oyster shell only found 2,000 miles north, in the warm waters along the coast of Ecuador. During the excavations Constanza carefully took notes on each discovery, which was no easy task in the cold and blustery conditions. At times the notepaper was almost ripped away by windblasts. Her meticulous notes describing the arrangement of the objects in gravesites later proved crucial in developing a better understanding of the capacocha ritual.

Before leaving the mountaintop, the team packed the mummies in dry ice to keep them frozen during the two-day trip to Catholic University of Salta. Over the next six years, Constanza, along with the help of other professionals, analyzed the frozen bodies. Their work determined that the younger girl was six, the boy was seven, and the older girl was 15 at the time they were sacrificed. Careful scrutiny of the younger girl revealed that she had been struck by lightning after her burial. Analysis of hair samples showed that during the last year of their lives the children had been fed on an enriched corn-based diet and had also ingested coca leaves, which contain a drug used to alleviate altitude sickness. The examination of artifacts and clothing indicated that the children had been transported from Cuzco, Peru. The journey from this city thousands of miles to the north would have taken months.

The mummies yielded the best-preserved ancient human DNA to date, which showed that none of the children were related to one another. Other evidence indicated the children were in good health before the sacrifices. CT scans identified that their internal organs were nearly perfect, and the fact that their bones showed no signs malnutrition signified that the children were from a high social class. This made sense, because it was known that many of the children sacrificed were usually those of local chiefs. It was thought to be an honor to the family when a child was chosen for sacrifice.

Along with all of these discoveries they even determined the cause of each child's death. The six-year-old girl had died from pulmonary edema, while the boy and the older girl had died from exposure to cold. Each mummy was placed in its own freezer at the Catholic University of Salta.

In 2001, after graduating with a doctorate degree, Constanza moved to a tiny village at the base of the Andes to manage a small archaeology museum. Here life was different from any place she had lived. Her home was a tiny adobe house. There were no televisions and only one phone in the entire hamlet.

Constanza was intrigued by the villagers' close connection to nature and respect for the Earth. She recognized that their festivities were similar to ones practiced by the Incas long ago. Many of the townsfolk moved 25 miles away to elevations of 13,000 to 14,000 feet to perform certain sacred ceremonies. Constanza felt at home in this peaceful, isolated pueblo. Later she regarded her years there as some of the most important in her life.

Constanza's childhood dream came true when she was hired not only as a professor of Incan archaeology but also as director of the Institute of High Mountain Research at Catholic University in Salta, Argentina. In Salta she was not far from Llullaillaco and other high mountains. Besides teaching and conducting

Constanza taking measurements atop a peak in the Andes.
Courtesy of Constanza Ceruti

research at the university, Constanza continued to explore the world's mountains. Over the years she has ascended more than 100 peaks higher than 16,500 feet (5,000 meters) in pursuit of high-elevation archaeological sites. She has also climbed mountains in the Canadian Rockies, the Sinai Peninsula, Greece, Italy, Mexico, Nepal, and Norway. In New Zealand she has visited mountains sacred to the Maori people and walked to the base of Mount Everest in winter. She has been honored with the Wings WorldQuest Courage Award and was the first woman to receive not only the Argentine Army's Gold Condor, but also the Archeological Institute of America's Indy Spirit Award, which honors scholar-adventurers who embody the character of the fictional archaeologist Indiana Jones.

Constanza believes in the sacredness of mountains and is driven by a passion to visit high-elevation archaeological sites before they are destroyed by treasure hunters and threatened by climate change. In her role as a National Geographic Emerging Explorer, she is committed to encouraging young people to explore. Undoubtedly her strong legs and lungs will allow her to explore many more high places in pursuit of people who reached these places before her.

Sophia Danenberg

REACHING THE HIGHEST SUMMIT

> *"It's [Everest] a very easy mountain to climb—that's why so many people do it. Technically, you just kind of walk up; it's not very hard. The problem is that it's so high, if anything whatsoever goes wrong, you're just dead. It's not really about having the ability to climb. It's about this ability to say, 'I can do it really well.'"* —Sophia Danenberg

As she approached the Mount Everest summit, a fierce, cold wind caused Sophia Dannenberg's oxygen mask to start clogging. She had never been at so high an elevation before, and her stuffed nose and mild case of bronchitis only made it more difficult to breathe. With each step the mask became more blocked. Despite Sophia's concerns about surviving the climb, she continued onward and upward to new heights.

Sophia Scott was born in 1972 in Homewood, Illinois, a southern suburb of Chicago where she was raised by her Japanese mother and African American father. Her parents were strictly the "indoorsy" types, so Sophia grew up without any experience hiking or camping. Living in the heart of the Midwest, she was hundreds of miles from the nearest high mountains, so the idea of climbing a peak was not something that young Sophia even considered doing. As a natural athlete, Sophia enjoyed playing basketball, but her hopes of excelling in the sport were dashed when she remained short in stature while her teammates continued to grow taller. Undaunted, she switched to running, an activity she could do well regardless of her height. In high school she competed on both the track and cross-country teams.

Besides being a talented athlete, Sophia was an exceptional student. In 1990, she was accepted to Harvard University in Cambridge, Massachusetts. There she joined other freshmen on her first backpacking trek sponsored by the Harvard Outing Club. For days, she and her fellow students carried heavy backpacks as they walked along trails in New Hampshire's rugged Presidential Range. At one point Sophia thought that she couldn't walk another step, but she only grew stronger. The literal high point of the trip was the summiting of her first peak.

At Harvard, Sophia majored in both environmental and public policy studies. After graduating in 1994, she was awarded a Fulbright Fellowship to study at Keio University in Japan. This led to a job for United Technologies managing energy and indoor air programs in Japan and China. Her next position with the company was at its headquarters in Hartford, Connecticut, working on green technology projects. When Sophia was 27, a childhood friend encouraged her to try rock climbing. Unlike basketball, height is not an issue with climbing. In fact, many of the top women rock climbers during that era were petite but muscular. With her natural ability, Sophia did well on her first climb. She quickly became enamored with the new sport, and on outings with the local chapter of the Appalachian Mountain Club, she developed new climbing skills. It was on one of these trips that she met a young man named David Danenberg, who was climbing with a friend in the same location.

"He was near the top of a cliff. He noticed me walking below," Sophia later explained to a journalist. David and Sophia were drawn to each other by their common passion for climbing and other outdoor activities. A few years after their chance meeting, they wed. Sophia Scott was now Sophia Scott Danenberg, and mountaineering became an important part of her married life. Their first major climb was in 2001 to the top of Tanzania's 19,000-foot-high Mount Kilimanjaro, the highest peak in Africa. Since then, she and David have traveled the world to climb. In 2002 Sophia ascended Mount Rainier and the glacier-mantled Mount Baker, both in Washington State. She and David then returned to East Africa to climb Mount Kenya. In 2005 she summited five peaks, including the highest peak in North America, Alaska's Mount McKinley; the second highest

Sophia's view of Mount Everest from below.
Courtesy of Wikimedia Commons

peak in New Zealand, Mount Tasman; and the towering Ama Dablam, known as Nepal's Matterhorn. Each peak taught her a new lesson. During each year of climbing she added new skills and developed her physical endurance.

"Each mountain I climbed I added a degree of difficulty, whether it was a higher altitude or even if it was lower, maybe adding something more technical. For example I climbed Mt. Kenya after I climbed Mt. Kilimanjaro. Mt. Kenya is a lot more technical climb," Sophia explained in an online interview.

In early 2006, Sophia gave notice to her employer that she wanted to take a three-month break during the coming spring. She wasn't planning to do anything spectacular, but she felt ready to climb higher than ever before. Sophia carefully considered ascending Cho Oyu, the world's sixth highest peak, located on the border of Nepal and Tibet. While investigating different guide services that lead trips there, one of the guides, Eric Simonson, became impressed by her attitude. He suggested that she might be ready for Mount Everest, also on the border of Nepal and Tibet and the planet's highest peak (29,029 feet). He said if she only made it as far as Camp Four, the highest camp on the route, she would still be higher than the summit of Cho Oyu.

"A lot of people seem driven by ego motives. I never got that from her. It was refreshing," Simonson remarked in an article about Sophia.

Sophia took his advice and signed up with an outfitter for an unguided climb. Without a guide, she and the other eight climbers on the trip would have to make their own decisions, such as choosing their exact route, when to make the last push for the summit, and when to turn back if there were problems. Sophia was comfortable with this arrangement because it allowed her to go at her own pace and to forgo the summit if it

Everest Base Camp even has a tea shop.
Courtesy of Wikimedia Commons

meant risking her life. As with the other climbers, she would be accompanied by two Sherpas. These local Himalayan villagers, known as some of the best professional porters and mountaineers, carry a portion of each climber's gear.

After many efforts by numerous expeditions up Everest, some resulting in death, New Zealander Sir Edmund Hillary and Tenzing Norgay, a Nepali, finally summited the peak in 1953. It was not until 22 years later that Japanese climber Junko Tabei became the first woman to accomplish this feat. Seven years later Marty Hoey died from a fall during her attempt to become the first American woman to reach the summit. Finally, in 1988, mountaineer Stacy Allison gained the distinction of being the first American woman to stand atop Everest. As each year passes, more and more climbers have reached the summit. In 2003 South African Sibusiso Vilane became the first African man to summit the world's tallest peak. So many people have gone up the mountain that at times Everest Base Camp looks like a tent city with trash issues.

On April 1, 2006, as 34-year-old Sophia Danenberg took her first steps up the lower slopes of Everest, no one, except family and friends, were aware that she might become the first African American to join company with other "firsts."

As Sophia climbed steadily upward, she was thankful to be in top physical shape. In the preceding year she had spent more time climbing than any time in the past. Unlike other mountains, the ascent into the thin atmosphere of the world's tallest mountain forces mountaineers to limit each day's climbing to short periods. Though this allows them to acclimate to the elevation, it makes the overall journey longer. Day after day of packing up gear and carrying it uphill into higher and higher altitudes is as much a mental as a physical challenge. The advantage of attempting this climb without any media coverage was that Sophia felt no pressure to succeed. She was perfectly aware that the mountain was in charge. With luck the weather would be good and her route would be avalanche free. One by one, she and the other climbers reached Camp I and then, at 21,300 feet, Camp II, also known as Advanced Base Camp. From there, using fixed ropes, Sophia ascended the Lhotse Face and finally reached the small ledge at 24,500 feet where Camp III is located, and where the atmosphere is extremely thin. After completing the next ascent of more than 1,600 feet, Sophia was very pleased to reach Camp IV.

"I wasn't sort of thinking, 'Yeah, I'm going to do this.' It was like, 'I'm going to see how it goes.' The goal was to get to Camp Four. The first time I really went, 'Jeez, I really want to do this,' was when I was making the decision to go for the summit," Sophia said afterward of the climb.

At this point the clock started ticking. At an elevation of 26,000 feet, climbers can only endure the thin air for two or three days at most. For this reason this last stopping point is referred to as the "death zone." A storm-caused delay can force mountaineers to retreat before they have the opportunity to summit. Sophia hoped to start for the top with her two Sherpas on summit day but woke up to bad weather. Knowing that they couldn't stay for long in the death zone, she decided to descend the next day. However, it was the mountain that had the final say.

"Between 7 PM and 10 PM the weather cleared. At 11 PM we made the decision to go for it," remembered Sophia. Using headlamps, she and her Sherpas, PaNuru and his brother, Mingma Tshiring, as well as many of the other climbers and their Sherpas, started for the summit. On their way up, Sophia, PaNuru, and Mingma passed some other climbers. When they got about halfway up, they halted at an overlook called the balcony. As Sophia looked down, she was surprised not to see the headlamps of any of the other mountaineers. She wondered if perhaps they had turned back for some reason. Maybe they knew another storm was developing. To ease her fear, she radioed camp and was told that no storms were expected but that Camp IV was still shrouded in clouds. Having ascended above the clouds, Sophia was treated to the sight of the starriest sky she perhaps would ever see. She knew that PaNuru and Mingma were under no obligation to summit if they didn't think it was safe. Their willingness to push upward gave Sophia the final confidence to reach the top.

As she neared the summit, her oxygen mask started clogging, making it difficult to breathe, which in combination with a case of bronchitis and frostbitten cheeks became a big issue.

"My first thought when I reached the top was honestly just surprise that I was there. Until the summit day I hadn't been as focused on getting to the top, and so it was just somewhat surprising once I actually got there. When I reached the summit, an ongoing problem I had had with my oxygen mask became a significant problem. Basically, it had been clogging, and it clogged completely once I was exposed to the wind that occurs when you reach the top and you don't have anything else blocking the wind.

"My second thought was, obviously, just needing to fix this blocked oxygen mask and get down. I don't even think I would have taken a photo if it had not been for PaNuru going, 'Nooo, you've got to take a photo, you've got to take a photo!' I was so focused on this mask problem," Sophia later recounted to a journalist.

"So I was like, 'Cool, I made it,'" Sophia later reflected in her understated way.

Sophia descended without any injuries except slightly frostbitten cheeks. She reached base camp by April 1 but was no April fool. She had been well prepared and unwilling to risk her life if conditions had deteriorated.

Three weeks later Sophia was at Disney World with her sister, niece, and nephew on a day when the amusement park was almost deserted due to a hurricane warning. It was only natural that they went on the newly opened ride Expedition Everest.

"On the real Mount Everest and on the Expedition Everest ride everybody always talks about the lines and the crowds. I was on both without the lines and the crowds," said Sophia.

Because Sophia hadn't blogged, gotten sponsors, nor contacted media before embarking on her Everest trip, no one knew that she had accomplished another Everest first. After news of her accomplishment was released, most people were surprised to find out she was the first African American to stand atop Everest. Other climbers, however, were aware that there have been few African American high-altitude mountaineers. In fact, Sophia had never met another black person on any big mountain. This is something she hopes to change as she becomes a role model for young people, especially girls.

By 2009 more than 2,500 people had reached Everest's summit. Most likely Sophia will not be the only African American to accomplish this feat. As she volunteers with groups such as Sierra Club Inner City Outings and speaks at schools, her message is clear. She tells young people that she was raised with the belief that most things are possible and that most dreams are achievable if, before dismissing them, you take time to figure out how to reach each goal. Maybe, for some of them, their goal will be to reach the highest summit.

PART II

SEEKING NATURE

Marianne North

PICTURING NATURE

> *"My horse was . . . very bony and old, with two great gaping wounds on her shoulders caused by the bites of vampire bats, into which the flies walked in the most distressing manner. After winding along two or three valleys, we began to mount in good earnest. The only danger on our path was from the hanging wreaths of bamboo and the acacia called cat's paw, which had been long untrimmed and might easily do serious damage to the faces of unwary travelers." —Marianne North*

Everyone warned Marianne North that the trip to the Brazilian state of Minas Gerais would be miserable, and some mentioned that a woman had recently died while traveling the same route. A Scotsman even told her there would be nothing of interest to see or paint—but not everyone could see through her artist's eyes. As for Marianne, the more people told her not to do something, the more determined she was to do it. As she rode a mule in the company of 36 other heavily laden mules, she skillfully navigated the rugged road, which she described as

Marianne poses at her easel in Ceylon (now Sri Lanka) for photographer Julia Cameron. *Courtesy of Wikimedia Commons*

having a "constant succession of holes and traps and pies of mud, often above a mule's knees."

With her mule's hooves encased in shoes of muck, Marianne lurched from side to side as if her mount were drunk. When the mule team reached a deep mud hole, the mules sank past their bellies and had to be hauled out by their heads and tails. Marianne not only accepted these hardships with a spirit of adventure, she also carefully observed the plants and animals they passed by in the lush Brazilian forest. She was fascinated by the sight of a candelabra tree with its razor-sharp leaves, a velvety pawed spider as large as a sparrow, and the many masses of exotic tropical flowers. In her baggage she carried her oil paints, brushes, and paper, with which she meticulously recorded all the new biological treasures she saw. On this journey, Marianne was at the start of many years of world travels—and on her way to becoming one of the most important botanical artists of the late 19th century.

Born on October 24, 1830, at Hastings Lodge on the south coast of Great Britain, Marianne North was the first daughter of Frederick North, a wealthy landowner and member of the British Parliament. Her mother, Janet North, had married Fredrick after the death of her first husband. Janet North's father, Marianne's granddad, was Sir John Majoribanks, also a Parliament member. Marianne's brother, Charles, was two years her senior; she also had an older half sister from her mother's first marriage.

As a youth, Marianne's father had left Great Britain for Switzerland to learn French and to trek in the Alps. When he became a father, he shared his love of travel and other cultures with his children, and he moved his family from place to place like migratory birds. During spring, London was home. In summer, it was a farmhouse in Roughham, Norfolk, where Marianne rode horses for hours each day. For part of each summer they traveled to Great Britain's northwest coast to stay at Gawthorpe Hall in Lancashire, the home Janet North inherited from her first husband. Marianne was happy with these seasonal migrations. This vagabond lifestyle allowed her to fashion her own schooling. Her parents and their educated friends were her informal teachers. Books by William Shakespeare, Sir Walter Scott, Daniel Defoe, and others, such as *Robinson Crusoe*, provided lessons in history, culture, geography, and adventure.

At age seven, Marianne was thrilled when her younger sister Catherine was born. During their youth Marianne, Charles, and Catherine grew up mingling with lords and ladies—but also with botanists such as George Bentham and Sir William Hooker and painters such as William Holman Hunt and Edward Lear. Hunt and Lear inspired Marianne to paint, and Bentham and Hooker sparked her interest in botany.

Sir William Hooker,
director of Kew Gardens.
*Courtesy of Wikimedia
Commons*

As a young woman, Mari-
anne discovered the joy of
painting. During the Victorian Age, painting was seen as
a suitable hobby for women
until they found the proper husband, but that would not be the
case with Marianne. Rather than painting being a hobby, painting would be her life's calling. Her close companionship with
her father allowed her to escape marriage—which she disdain-
fully described as being a "terrible experiment" and referred to
being a wife as "a sort of upper servant."

Marianne and her father were kindred spirits. "He was from
first to last the one idol and friend of my life, and apart from him
I had little pleasure and no secrets," Marianne said of her father.

When Marianne was 16, she and her family spent eight
months in Germany. They then traveled around Europe for the
next two years. In 1850, when Marianne was 20, she took lessons
in flower painting from a Dutch artist, and the following year
she studied with another instructor.

Five years later, Marianne's mother fell gravely ill. When
she was near death, she requested that Marianne look after her
father. Janet North's death was a blow to the whole family, especially Fredrick. After he was reelected to Parliament, he moved
the family to London. Charles was at college, and though Marianne was now mistress of the household, she devoted as much

time as she could to her newly discovered passion for painting flowers. She often visited the Royal Botanic Gardens at Kew directed by Sir William Hooker, a family friend. In this vast garden she had her choice of plants to depict in her paintings. The tropical species were her favorites. At these gardens she met William Hooker's son, Joseph, who was well known for his botanical expeditions to Antarctica and the Himalayas. And through Joseph she was introduced to Charles Darwin.

At this point in her life, Marianne spent her summers with her father and sister, Catherine, exploring Spain, Switzerland, Greece, and other corners of Europe. As was their custom, Fredrick North and each of his daughters had a sketchbook and diary. Marianne excelled at both sketching and writing. After nine years this summer routine changed: Catherine married, and Fredrick North lost his seat in Parliament. Marianne and her father began traveling to more exotic locales throughout the year. They wintered in Egypt and in the spring trekked through Syria, where Marianne produced an impressive number of watercolors. She was developing a unique and controversial style of accurate renderings of plants pictured in their actual habitats, including the birds, butterflies, or other animals native to each place. These were unlike most botanical illustrations, which simply illustrated the plant as if it grew in a pot.

During the Christmas holidays in 1868, an Australian artist stayed as their guest at Hastings Lodge and gave Marianne lessons in oil painting. This new medium felt right to Marianne; she described it as being "almost impossible to leave off once it gets possession of one."

The next summer, while she traveled with her father in Austria, he fell ill, and shortly after they returned home to Hastings, he passed away. Marianne was overcome by this loss; she had lost her closest companion. For the first time in her life she was by herself. At 39 years old she was now faced with the choice of either living as an "old maid" in Hastings or pursuing her dream of traveling the world and painting. As soon as she chose a life of adventure, Marianne knew it was the right one for her. Without a husband, she had no one telling her what she could or could not do, and her inheritance left her wealthy enough to live her life as she wished. But women of her class were expected to be chaperoned while traveling. That winter she journeyed to Sicily accompanied by her maid, but she felt it was constraining. She swore to never have a chaperone again, explaining, "I am a very wild bird and like liberty."

When back in Great Britain, Marianne sold Hastings Lodge. She then accepted an invitation from a wealthy American widow, whom she and her father had met in Egypt, to visit her in Boston. There she met the young botanist Charles Sargent, who soon after was appointed as the first director of Harvard University's Arnold Arboretum. Her new paintings of North American botany included a portrait of a twisted old red cedar growing on a rocky bluff and a luxurious composition featuring rare lady's slipper orchids, jack-in-the-pulpits, and other American blossoms. After visiting and painting scenes at Niagara Falls, she traveled to Washington, DC. At the White House she had an audience with President Ulysses Grant and the First Lady, during which she was treated royally, because they mistakenly thought she was the daughter of the former prime minister of Britain, who was also named North.

Finally Marianne boarded a steamer in New York bound for Jamaica. On the island she lived for a month in a house surrounded by an old, deserted, overgrown botanic garden. In her journal she stated that she was "in a state of ecstasy" as she created one painting after another of the rich tropical vegetation. Her only companions for the entire month were her Jamaican cook and gardener. True to her character, Marianne was as happy in the company of a poor farmer as she was with a person of wealth.

Her next trip was to Brazil. In Rio de Janeiro, she boarded a mule tram at six o'clock each morning to go to the botanical garden, where she painted all day. She arrived back at her hotel at sunset. She watched monkeys and a sloth in the hills above the city. On one stroll she met a Mr. Gordon and his daughter, Mary, who invited her to come stay with them in Minas Gervais, a Brazilian province.

The journey to their home in Minas was long but fascinating. Her room there overlooked a lush tropical garden. Here for the first time she saw "sensitive" plants, such as a mimosa, which fold their leaves closed when touched, as well as tiny hummingbird nests suspended with silk from the tips of enormous leaves. Inspired by this setting, she created one painting after another, both of close-up images of blossoms and landscapes of tropical forests.

In 1875 Marianne began a journey around the world during which she painted flora in California, Japan, Borneo, Java, and Ceylon (now Sri Lanka). One of her first stops in California was Yosemite National Park, where she visited the Mariposa Grove of Giant Sequoias. "I had a long day's work in that lovely forest painting the huge tree called the Great Grisly, whose first side branch is as big as any trunk in Europe," Marianne wrote. On another day in the grove she completed a painting of the red, waxy-looking snow plant, a species that lacks green leaves because it obtains nutrients from fungi instead of from the sun.

Marianne described the stagecoach driver who took her and her friends to Yosemite Valley as a "villainous-looking bandit." He took a liking to her because of her lack of concern for bears and gave her some rattlesnake tails.

Marianne departed from San Francisco in October aboard a luxurious steamer bound for Japan. During her tour of Japan, she created a painting of Mount Fuji. Unlike those composed by Japanese artists that focus on the famous mountain, in her painting the snowcapped peak serves as a backdrop for her portrait of delicate wisteria blossoms.

In the beginning of 1876 she continued onward to Singapore and next visited Sarawak, on the island of Borneo. There she traveled many leagues upriver on a boat and 15 miles on a pony, sometimes crossing steep ravines over "cranky poles." She described the forest as a "world of wonders" with misty mountains, towering trees, and "huge black apes." She painted a species of lily from this area so accurately that it was later recognized by botanists as a new species, which was named *Crinum northianum* in her honor. Another painting of a strange-looking pitcher plant with flowers resembling jugs was also new to science and would be named *Nepenthes northiana*. Yet another plant name commemorating her discovery is *Areca northiana*, a species of feather palm.

During the next stop of this world tour, she visited Ceylon, where the famous photographer Julia Margaret Cameron photographed

Nepenthes northiana, one of the many species named for Marianne.
Courtesy of Wikimedia Commons

The Marianne North Gallery at Kew Gardens.
Courtesy of Wikimedia Commons

Marianne at her easel. After a year in India she finally returned
home. In London an exhibition of her art received rave reviews.
By now her paintings numbered in the hundreds and took up
too much space in her home. She offered Joseph Hooker, now
the director of Kew Gardens, both her paintings and funds for a
gallery to display them in. He was only too happy to accept this
gift. Marianne then hired an architect, who had new ideas about
illuminating art galleries with natural light, to draw up plans.

By 1880, Marianne was ready for another adventure, and
Charles Darwin suggested that she paint the unique plants of
Australia and New Zealand. Throughout the diary accounts of
her travels Marianne wrote of oven-like temperatures, drench-
ing rainstorms, travel sickness, leeches, and squalid lodgings,
but she never complained of these hardships. However, it was the

cold, wet weather of New Zealand's South Island that brought on rheumatic pain about which Marianne finally complained.

The Marianne North Gallery was due to open in 1882. Marianne wanted tea and coffee service there, but Hooker vetoed this idea. He reminded her that her gallery would be a place of study and contemplation, not an amusement park. In her determined way Marianne managed to have coffee and tea at her gallery by painting tea and coffee plants above the entrance door. On opening day, 832 of her paintings were arranged in a tightly packed display. They were grouped according to the place in the world each plant is from, making a complete viewing of her art a quick tour of six continents.

In 1883, Marianne visited South Africa; among her many paintings was one more new species that would be named for her, an aloe plant sometimes known as a red hot poker, *Kniphofia northiana*. Then on her trip to the Seychelles Islands off the East African coast she painted a capuchin tree that botanists later named *Northea seychellana*.

For more than 20 years Marianne had tirelessly created pictures of the Earth's plants and animals. Many of the plants she painted are extinct today, falling victim to what her friend Joseph Hooker had referred to as "the axe and the forest fire, the plough, and the flock." Just shy of her 60th birthday, her indomitable energy, like a fading comet, was spent. Marianne passed away with her sister, Catherine, by her side, leaving a visual record of her adventures for all to see.

Martha Maxwell

EXPLORING WILDLIFE IN THE ROCKIES

> *"She would crawl though underbrush, over rocks, up mountains, and down streams until she found her quarry. Then she would stand infinitely patient, silent as a tree, watching the birds and animals."* —Mabel Maxwell, Martha's daughter

In 1868, only a few months after geologist John Wesley Powell and his party made the first recorded ascent of Colorado's Longs Peak, Martha Maxwell was searching for wildlife in a nearby mountain valley called Middle Park. Settled in a campsite with her 10-year-old daughter Mabel; husband, James; and half sister Mary, she blissfully investigated the mountain wildlife and savored the magnificent scenery.

"Clothes damp, boots hard and stiff, frost a quarter of an inch thick on everything outside the tent, and no hope of warmth or breakfast, till from under sheltering rocks and logs enough fuel can be gathered for a fire," Mary later wrote of their experience.

For Martha, who had lived in a log cabin and traveled cross-country in a wagon, these were hardly discomforts. What did cause worry was an accident that occurred as she and Mabel were traveling home. Martha was riding a horse with Mabel seated behind her. With one of her hands Mabel held the reins of their pack mule, which was following behind. While they were crossing a steep slope, the mule bolted and pulled Mabel off the horse. Fortunately a boulder on the slope blocked her fall; otherwise she would have tumbled down the precipitous hillside to her death.

Martha was no stranger to death or hardship. Following Martha's birth on July 21, 1831, her mother, Amy Sanford Dartt, was bedridden for many years. Their home was Dartt's Settlement, Pennsylvania, a small community named after Martha's great-grandfather. When she was only two years old, Martha's father, Spencer Dartt, caught scarlet fever and died. Still bedridden, her mother was incapable of taking care of Martha and the farm. Abigail Sanford, Martha's grandmother, came to the rescue; she moved from Connecticut to care for her daughter and young granddaughter. Abigail was strong-willed, independent, and loving. Martha adored her. Together they rambled in the forest and marveled at the squirrels, turtles, birds, and other creatures they saw there.

Two years later, Martha's mother was still an invalid. Grandmother Abigail decided that it was time to go to Connecticut to seek a cure. Martha, now four years old, was heartbroken at being left behind in the care of her father's relatives. It was a long, lonely year for Martha, but at its end Grandmother Abigail returned with Martha's mother finally in good health. With Martha's help Amy could now care for the farm. Between school and work at home, Martha became both self-reliant and passionate about learning.

Just a few months after Martha's 10th birthday, Amy remarried. Her new husband was Josiah Dartt, a cousin of Martha's father. At 23 years old, he was 13 years younger than Amy and

13 years older than Martha. Josiah was a kind and devout man as well as a lover of books and nature. Within a year, in December 1841, Martha's baby sister Mary was born. Martha adored her little sister and became her main caregiver when their mother fell ill again.

Both Josiah and Amy shared a desire to be missionaries and dreamed of converting Native Americans in the West. In pursuit of this dream, the family headed off for Oregon in a covered wagon in August 1844. Along with them went Grandma Abigail and three of her adult sons. Mary was 20 months old, and Amy was again pregnant. For Martha the trip was a grand adventure.

"We went by land and lived in our wagons night and day. I never enjoyed five weeks better I think," Martha later recalled.

In October they stopped in Byron, Illinois, to stay with Abigail's husband, Grandfather Sanford, who had moved from Connecticut to live with another one of her mother's brothers there. Abigail and some other family members came down with malaria. Martha, who was one of the few who remained healthy, took on the responsibility of caring for the sick. All recovered—except Grandma Abigail, who, despite Martha's efforts, passed away that fall. This was a terrible loss for Martha as well as the rest of the family. Born into this mourning family was Martha's newest sister, Elizabeth, who Martha took care of in addition to little Mary.

In spring the family traveled north to Baraboo, Wisconsin, where they were guests of Martha's uncle, Joseph Sanford, until they moved into a simple little cabin on the outskirts of town. Here Martha took on the duties of a mother as she labored on the farm and looked after her baby sisters. One day while Josiah was off working, Martha noticed a rattlesnake on the cabin floor. It was coiled up just a few feet away from Mary. Without hesitation Martha grabbed her father's gun and skillfully shot the snake. Her keen vision and good marksmanship would serve her well in the coming years.

Martha hoped to attend college. She wished for a career instead of a life of farming and housework. In the early 1850s, few women received training for a profession. Fortunately for Martha, there were now colleges that accepted women students, and her parents supported her wish for schooling. Though the family had little money, Josiah scraped together enough funds to send Martha to Oberlin College in Ohio. For Martha, being at college was a "continual feast" for her mind. She studied hard, earning the attention of the college president for her efforts. She befriended other students, both male and female. She wanted to study science, but her hopes were dashed. Martha's parents had run out of money for tuition, so she returned home.

Unknown to her family, Martha and a male schoolmate had developed a mutual affection. At home Martha daydreamed about continuing her education and waited patiently to hear from her beau. Meanwhile, another opportunity to attend college arrived. James Maxwell, a well-to-do Baraboo businessman and a widower with six children, was seeking someone to chaperone his two oldest children at Lawrence University in Appleton, Wisconsin. He approached Martha to ask if she would take on this task and promised that if she did, he would pay her fees for courses at the university. Martha agreed to these terms and continued her studies at the new school.

Months went by without a word from Martha's young suitor. Then, out of the blue, she received a letter from James Maxwell, confessing his love for her and proposing marriage. He was a man 20 years her senior who had children not much younger than she. Though he was a prosperous businessman, she was in love with another man her own age. She had no idea what to do. Not wanting to make a decision, she wrote back to James telling him that she had to discuss his proposal with her mother. Meanwhile, Martha anxiously waited for a letter from her Oberlin sweetheart.

Having not heard from her sweetheart, she agreed to marry James. When she returned home after the wedding, a letter awaited her. It was from her sweetheart. It had been sent a month before and been lost in the mail. In it he expressed his hope "that soon he could claim her for life." Unfortunately, Martha was already claimed. She was distraught, but as was her fashion, she tried to make the best of what life dealt her. It would not be easy. Within three years, James lost his businesses due to unwise decisions. All that remained of his former fortune was their house. Martha, who had cared for the Maxwell children, was now pregnant and faced with poverty. Within two years of giving birth to their daughter, Mabel, the financial situation was even worse. She and James had to do something.

Like others with financial problems, Martha and James boldly decided to seek their fortune out West in the newly discovered goldfields of Colorado. Thinking the journey would be too dangerous for young Mabel, James and Martha left her behind with her grandparents, Josiah and Amy. Thus family history repeated itself. However, unlike Martha's one-year separation from her mother, Mabel wouldn't see Martha or James for several years.

By the time they arrived in Nevadaville, Colorado, it was too late for easy pickings. James found a job driving cattle from the plains to Colorado, and Martha opened a boardinghouse. Determined to have more control of their finances, she worked long hours and invested her earnings in a mine and land. From afar Martha gazed at the beauty of the mountains that she could see from town and dreamed of exploring them.

Once more misfortune struck: a fire swept through town. Most of the buildings went up in flames, including her boarding house. But this disaster led to an encounter that forever changed her life. She and James decided to move into a cabin on the land Martha had purchased. After being away from home for a few days, they returned to discover that three men had claimed it. One of them was a German taxidermist. Strangely, frontier law allowed settlers to claim "unoccupied" homes. Martha and James convinced two of the men to leave, but the German refused to budge. She was intrigued by his stuffed specimens of mountain animals and offered to pay him to teach her his craft. Again, the German stubbornly refused her wishes. Martha then figured she could use his own tactics to evict him. She patiently watched the cabin from a hidden lookout post for several days. When the German left on an errand she quickly removed the lock on the door and replaced it with her own. As she carried out his possessions she carefully examined the stuffed animal specimens and the supplies and tools he used to make them. It was at that moment Martha suddenly realized that she had found the kind of profession she had been seeking. Now all that remained was to find someone to train her.

In 1864, when Martha arrived back in Wisconsin, Mabel was six years old and hardly knew her mother. In addition to resuming her role as a mother, Martha took lessons from a local man who knew a little about taxidermy. Then Martha perfected her new skills by assisting a professor at Baraboo's new college in assembling a collection of stuffed animals. At first Martha was dissatisfied with her specimens. The skins were too loose for the frames. Through trial and error she discovered that if she molded the frame in plaster, the stuffed animal would look more natural. The displays she created of each animal's natural habitat made each specimen appear even more real. People viewing her specimens could now imagine how the animal looked in the wild.

In 1868 Martha returned to Colorado with Mabel. They traveled most of the way by train. Martha realized that the West was rapidly transforming. She noticed that as the number of settlers increased, the numbers of wild animals declined. Now was the time, Martha figured, to document the wealth of wildlife by making a scientific collection of the animals before they were gone. At the beginning of her project, she paid boys to bring her specimens, but she soon found that she could do it better herself. Sometimes she took Mabel with her on collecting trips in the mountains. At other times she ventured off alone dressed in a practical but unorthodox outfit. One journalist described her hunting attire as a "thick frock falling below the knee, a tight-fitting jacket with rolling collar, beneath which passed a handkerchief tied in sailor fashion, stout laced shoes going well to the knee, and any kind of head-gear that happened to be within reach; with a large netted and fringed game bag hanging over her right shoulder, a powder-flask, a double-barrel fowling piece, and a well-trained dog."

Martha's calling card shows her dressed for hunting.
Courtesy of Beverly Wilgus

Martha pursued her prey fearlessly, often risking her life. On one occasion she was trapped within a herd of bison, but she managed to shoot the one she wanted and escaped unharmed. On another hunting trip Martha trekked high up on a mountainside in pursuit of a white-tailed ptarmigan and was caught in a thunderstorm with lightning striking all around her. Again she survived unscathed.

Despite having little space to work in the family's two-room stone house in Boulder, Martha managed to prepare dozens of specimens. In the fall of 1868 she displayed her work at the annual exhibition of the Colorado Agricultural Society. The *Rocky Mountain News* reported that hers was the largest collection of birds from the Rocky Mountains region ever exhibited. More than 100 species of stuffed bird skins were arranged on the branches of two large shrubs. Martha earned praise for her skill as a taxidermist as well as her contributions to science. She was awarded both of the exhibition's top honors as well as a $50 cash prize.

At this time Boulder was far from any library that had the books Martha needed to identify each species in her collection. She wrote to the Smithsonian Institution in Washington, DC, for help, and Joseph Henry, the Smithsonian's secretary, replied with an offer to identify any specimens she sent him. He also put her in contact with Smithsonian scientist Spencer Fullerton Baird.

After many years, James Maxwell was finally successful enough with his business to purchase a new brick home for his family, but their residence there was short-lived. When a Methodist minister cheated James out of his investments, they again lost their home. Martha was now more determined than ever to find a way to support herself and Mabel.

Her next exhibit at the agricultural fair in 1870 contained about 600 specimens. One reporter noted that it contained "nearly every bird and beast of this country, with many of the reptiles." Best of all it was one of the most popular exhibits. Martha decided to sell this impressive collection to Shaw's Garden in Saint Louis, later known at the Missouri Botanical Garden. With her earnings she purchased land in Boulder Canyon and immediately began assembling a new collection. Within three years she had enough specimens to open the Rocky Mountain Museum. Housed in a building on Boulder's main street, each exhibit featured lifelike animal specimens set in displays resembling their natural habitats. News of this amazing woman hunter and taxidermist who had created her own museum exhibits spread far and wide. Visitors flocked to the museum and gladly paid the twenty-five-cent admission.

In 1874 Martha sent two bird skins to Baird at the Smithsonian. He was pleased to hear from her and sent her publications about birds and mammals. This led to Martha's ongoing professional relationship with the country's foremost scientific institution, which developed further when Baird's coworker Robert Ridgway asked Martha to procure birds for him. Ridgway had begun collecting birds at the young age of 16 while serving for two years as a member of one of western America's most important expeditions, the survey of the 40th parallel. Later in life he would become the lead ornithologist at the Smithsonian, a post he held for more than half a century. Martha was thrilled to assist him. When she sent him a unique owl specimen, he verified that it was a subspecies of eastern screech owl and named it in her honor. Martha proved to be an astute and tireless explorer, finding wildlife where few scientists had ventured. A black-footed ferret she collected and preserved confirmed the existence of this rare mammal that had previously only been described by naturalist John James Audubon.

The black-footed ferret was one of the animals that Martha confirmed the
presence of in Colorado.
Courtesy of Wikimedia Commons

With Mabel now attending Oberlin College, Martha needed
to earn more money to pay for tuition. She moved her museum
to Denver to increase visitation. Here in the state capital her
work was even more appreciated and led to an offer she dared
not refuse. The Colorado state legislature asked her to exhibit
her collection in the Colorado pavilion at the upcoming 1876
Centennial Exhibition in Philadelphia. This was the United
States' first official World's Fair, where there would be millions
of visitors. Martha was offered free transport of her specimens
and displays as well as a salary. Martha accepted the offer. Now
she had the money to pay for the remainder of Mabel's college
costs.

Martha's display of wildlife of the western plains and mountains at the Centennial Exhibition was her most realistic and
elaborate yet. In one section there was a mountain scene with

Martha in front of her exhibit at the Centennial Exposition.
Courtesy of the Bridgeman Art Library, NYC

trees, boulders, and a stream trickling down into a small lake with "swimming" fish and "sunning" turtles, and beavers, muskrats, and water birds along the shore. Above the lake on the "mountain" was a cave with a grizzly bear, along with a mountain sheep and, farther up, a puma. One reporter wrote of a woman who was so taken in by the magic of Martha's work that she collected water from the stream in a small bucket and offered it to friends, believing it was truly Colorado mountain water and not from the Philadelphia tap that it really was.

Martha was a celebrity. Seated in front the display of stuffed antelope, elk, enormous bison, prairie dogs, and rattlesnakes, she was a striking figure. Everyone wanted to know all about her and her adventures. They wondered how this petite and sweet-voiced woman had accomplished all her work. Martha was gratified by people's response. Beyond this she was happy to be an example for other women by demonstrating what women are capable of accomplishing. Many visitors to the Centennial

Exhibition considered her display one of the highlights of the entire exposition. With as many as one out of five Americans making their way there, Martha's work was viewed by an enormous number of people.

Sadly, after the event was over, Martha never returned to her beloved Rocky Mountains. She developed an infection and died unexpectedly shortly before her 50th birthday. In her short lifetime she had overcome difficulties that would have stopped less ambitious and persistent individuals from pursuing their dreams. Martha's achievements made her a model for others willing to step beyond the boundaries of their time.

Ynes Mexia

IN PURSUIT OF UNKNOWN FLORA

> *"I found the luxuriance of the vegetation actually embarrassing. It was hard to know where to begin to collect and still harder to know when to stop."* —Ynes Mexia

At 55 years old, Ynes Mexia ventured off to western Mexico with renowned botanist Roxana Ferris. This was her first plant-collecting adventure, and as the daughter of a Mexican father, Ynes was fluent in Spanish and familiar with Mexican culture. This was helpful to Ferris, but even better were Ynes's collecting skills. Ynes possessed a sharp eye for identifying plants and the ability to efficiently prepare specimens. Halfway through the expedition, Ynes tumbled off a cliff, injuring a hand and breaking some of her ribs. She was unable to collect any more specimens on the expedition. Fortunately, she had already collected 500 plant species, several of which were new to science. One species was even named *Mimosa mexiae* in her honor. Unfazed by her accident, Ynes was anxious for another adventure—she had discovered a passion for exploring the unknown.

Ynes preparing plant specimens
while in the field.
California Academy of Science

Ynes was born on May 24, 1870, in Washington, DC, to a Mexican diplomat, Enrique Antonio Mexia, and Sarah R. Wilmer, an American divorcee with six children from her previous marriage. Ynes's grandfather, José Antonio Mexia, had been an important Mexican politician and general. He was executed in 1839 after being involved in an attempted uprising against President Antonio López de Santa Anna. While Ynes was still young, her parents separated, and she moved with her mother and siblings to a vast ranch in Texas that belonged to the Mexia family. Here Ynes learned to ride horses and explore the outdoors. She had little formal schooling until she returned, at age 15, to Maryland to attend a Catholic girls' academy. During her two years of studies there, she frequently visited a nearby convent and contemplated becoming a nun. At age 18 she instead chose to live at her father's hacienda in Mexico City, where she stayed for the next 20 years. Over these years both her parents passed away and she inherited part of her father's estate. She wed a German-Spanish merchant who died after only six years of marriage. Ynes then started a successful poultry business, and only four years later, at 38, she married again. This time her husband was only 22 years old. The marriage was a grave mistake that left Ynes emotionally distraught.

Ynes divorced, sold her business, and moved to San Francisco, California, where she sought help for her psychological condition. It is hard to believe that Ynes, who for the next 10 years would suffer periods of extreme emotional instability, would one day become one of the most remarkable explorers of her time.

At the age of 50 Ynes began going on hikes with the Sierra Club, and her life blossomed. The hiking, the company of others with a love of the outdoors, and the richness of plant life she saw on these treks all contributed to improving her physical and emotional health. After taking a summer field class at Pacific Grove, California, with Stanford University botanist Leroy Abrams, Ynes discovered her life's mission. Abrams was the curator of the university's plant collection, and through him she met his assistant curator, Roxana Ferris. Thus began Ynes's adventures as a plant collector with Roxana in Mexico.

Upon her return from the first expedition, Ynes enrolled in another field class, this time at the University of California at Berkeley. There she befriended N. Floy Bracelin, who was an assistant curator at the University of California Herbarium, and met Dr. William Setchell, head of the university's botany department. William was impressed by the wide array of plant specimens Ynes had collected in Mexico. He provided her with funds and a gold seal of approval from the university to show Mexican officials. N. Floy Bracelin, also known as Bracie, offered to help catalog future specimens.

In September 1926 Ynes embarked from San Francisco aboard the Pacific Mail steamship bound for Mázatlan on Mexico's Pacific Coast. This was the start of a seven-month journey through remote areas in several Mexican states. In each region Ynes hired local guides, known as *mozos*. One of them, Mauro, used his lasso to collect figs growing high up in a native species of fig tree growing in the mountains. Another *mozo*, named Juan, led her on an obscure trail up Cerro de San Juan, where she noticed a shrub she had never seen before. Juan called it *pie de pajaro*, Spanish for "bird's foot." Ynes collected some specimens, and it turned out to be yet one more species previously unknown to botanists. Ynes also searched for plants from the comfort of a dugout canoe in the delta of Rio San Pedro. At the river's mouth, along the edge of oil-nut palm groves, she discovered a sunflower-like shrub more than six feet tall. This new species was later named *Zemenia mexiae* in her honor. In the mountains near Puerto Vallarta, her guide's face and hands became badly swollen with a rash that lasted a whole week after collecting leaves of a tree in the same plant family as poison oak and ivy, but Ynes was unaffected by the toxic foliage. While following a steep, forested trail in a range of volcanic mountains, Ynes noticed a shrub with small globe-like flowers. This plant turned out to be another one unknown to scientists. It was not only a new species, but also a new genus: *Mexianthus mexicanus* would be the first plant with a genus named in her honor.

"The collecting was very good, but oh! The animated nature. I was introduced to . . . infant ticks, about the size of the dot in the letter *i*. There was all the collecting in the world and the streams and wood were beautiful, so I enjoyed my stay despite the bugs," Ynes later wrote in an article about her journey.

Years earlier Ynes had been overweight, out of shape, and directionless. Now, she explored steep mountains and seaside cliffs, both on foot and horseback. She stayed in rugged campsites and once even set up her cot in a woodcutter's banana patch where mountain lions had recently killed two of his dogs.

By the end of her travels in April 1927, she had collected a remarkable 33,000 specimens, one of which belongs to a new genus, and 50 that were new species. For a new botanist it was remarkable to have one genus and seven species named after her. This accomplishment was only possible because Ynes had the remarkable ability to remember the vast number of plants she had seen in botanic gardens and in the field. This enabled her to notice plants that were new to her.

In 1928, Ynes headed north to collect plants in Alaska. This was followed by another collecting journey in northern Mexico later that same year. In October 1929 Ynes boarded a steamer to Brazil for an extensive exploration of that country's flora. First she investigated the highlands, where she stayed for a year and a half. On one expedition, botanist Mary Agnes Chase, a specialist in grasses, joined her. They might have made a dynamic team, but they didn't get along well together. Both were bright, headstrong, self-taught botanists, but each preferred different modes of travel. Ynes enjoyed "roughing it" by riding on horseback and camping out. Agnes would rather travel by train and stay in hotels.

On August 28, 1931, Ynes embarked on her greatest adventure. Her plan was to traverse South America at its widest point. She had an entire truckload of equipment loaded aboard a river steamer on which she traveled up the Amazon. To Ynes, its vast width made it seem more like an inland sea than a river. With a screened cabin, electric fans, an ice-making machine, and fresh meat in the form of live cattle, for Ynes it felt like a luxurious journey. As they chugged upriver Ynes sighted enormous caimans sliding off sandbanks, flocks of parakeets, and dugout canoes everywhere, ferrying passengers and produce. When the ship sidled up to the bank so the crew could collect fodder for the hungry cattle, Ynes would join them.

"I jump into boots and khaki (much to the amusement of the passengers) and walk the plank to investigate the forest," Ynes wrote in her account of the journey.

After 24 days and 2,500 miles traveling up the river, they reached Iquitos, Peru. Here Ynes repacked her gear, laid in several months' worth of supplies, and hired three guides. Aboard a launch they traveled up the Marañón River to Barranca, Peru, where she then boarded a large dugout canoe paddled by four indigenous Peruvians. To reach the upper river, they had to paddle through the Pongo de Manseriche, a five-mile-long gorge bound by 2,000-foot-high vertical walls that in some places were only 100 feet apart. Once through this awesome cleft, they set up camp at the mouth of Rio Santiago just in time for the rainy season to begin. For the next three months this was both Ynes's home and scientific field station. She explored the river and its tributary by canoe. She climbed to the crest of the Sierra del Pongo. Week by week, her plant collection grew and grew. Also growing was the volume of water in the river, making it impossible to return to Iquitos via canoe. Undaunted, Ynes persuaded her crew to built a large raft out of balsa wood logs. On her wild journey downriver the raft was "tossed about like a straw" and caught in a giant whirlpool, which "whirled us around thrice, then spewed us out." Ynes later said of the raft, "while the smoke was annoying when the raft drifted tail first, that was the only drawback to the most delightful mode of transportation I have encountered."

As she continued her journey downriver on the raft she jotted down notes, observed river birds, and prepared her collections, despite interruptions from a baby monkey that insisted on being petted.

In Iquitos, Ynes packed up her collection for shipment to California before hopping onto a hydroplane up the Amazon. She continued her cross-continent journey via airplane, mule, automobile, and finally train to Lima and onward to the Pacific Coast. By the time she returned to San Francisco in March 1932, she had accumulated more than 65,000 specimens.

From September 1934 through January 1937, Ynes again searched for plants in South America. She collected specimens from Ecuador in the north all the way down to Tierra del Fuego on the southern tip of the continent and brought home another 20,000 specimens. All this time Ynes was unaware that she was ill. She departed on one more Mexican adventure, and less than two months after returning to California, Ynes died from lung cancer. Just 12 years before, she had been a novice botanist. Today she is remembered as one of the most skilled and prolific plant collectors of the 20th century, who added more to our knowledge of the botanical diversity of both Mexico and South America than any plant collector before or since. The 150,000 specimens she collected reside in the most important herbariums of the world, and the numerous species named in her honor are the legacy of this woman who began exploring plants so late in her life.

Ynes in the saddle, a common sight on her expeditions.
California Academy of Science

Margaret Lowman

LIFE IN THE TREETOPS

> *"The village shaman said that if the spirits were willing to allow us to climb this tree, we could; the very first line went up and over the branch, a sign that the spirits looked favorably on our conservation project."* —Margaret Lowman

As Meg Lowman stepped into the gully in an Australian rain forest, it seemed as if the ground near her feet was moving. Looking down, she realized that she had almost stepped on an Australian brown snake. Worse yet, only a few feet ahead she noticed a slithering mass of the extremely venomous and aggressive serpents. Had she been transported to an Indiana Jones movie? Little by little, Meg backed away until she was safe. After calming down she decided it would be best to select another location for her study of the forest canopy.

In Elmira, New York, where Meg grew up, she explored nearby forests and fields with her best friend, Betsy Hilfiger. Together they discovered insects, box turtles, and other creatures. They scrambled up trees and built forts while Betsy's brother Tommy stitched bell-bottom jeans in their family's base-ment. In fifth grade, Meg won second prize for her flower col-lection at the New York State Science Fair. This was an unusual accomplishment in the early 1960s, an era when few girls were encouraged to study science.

Meg developed an interest in birds and joined the local Audu-bon Society chapter, but she was the only member under 65 years old. She wrote to the head of the Audubon Society asking if there was any group for young bird watchers. He kindly replied and suggested she attend a nature study camp in the backwoods of West Virginia. It was here that Meg found her first mentor, John Trott, who was an enthusiastic naturalist and codirected the camp with his wife. The other campers were mostly from Washington, DC, where they benefited from special courses at the Smithsonian Institution. At a time in her life when Meg may have felt alone in her passion, she now spent each summer with a community of other teens who shared her curiosity and love of nature.

In 1972, Meg enrolled at Williams College in Williamstown, Massachusetts. She was drawn to its wooded campus and strong science program. The previously all-male college had just started admitting women, and male students outnumbered females five to one. Meg studied biology with a focus on trees and did well enough in this mostly male world to graduate cum laude (with honors).

When the opportunity came to earn a master's degree in ecology at the University of Aberdeen, in Scotland's north coun-try, Meg was anxious to explore the forests in a different part of the world. Her experience with winters in upstate New York, however, did nothing to prepare her for the frigid temperatures of winters in the far north. Her low-rent student lodgings were unheated, so she sat wrapped in an electric blanket while she studied, and she piled on every bit of clothing she had during her research outdoors.

In high latitudes, birches are common forest trees, and it was the leaves of these trees that Meg observed through the seasons for her master's thesis. After she earned her degree, one of her professors suggested that she pursue doctoral studies of the tropical rain forest in Australia. This made sense to Meg, who was more than ready to abandon the chilly north for a warmer climate.

As luck would have it, a chance meeting with a professor from Australia led to her being offered a fellowship. Meg looked forward to investigating the biologically diverse Australian forests but had no clue that she would be on the cutting edge of a new field of ecology.

At Williams College, Meg had learned to succeed in a primarily male community, but this had not prepared her for the much more conservative atmosphere in Australia, where she was one of only two female PhD students at the University of Sydney. It was 1978, but it seemed like 1958 when the head of the biology department asked Meg why she was studying for a doctorate instead of just getting married. The university was still very much a man's world.

Fortunately, Meg's academic adviser believed in her. He suggested that she investigate the foliage in the rain forest in the treetops, also called the canopy. Scientists had many questions, such as how many years an evergreen leaf could stay alive in the rain forest.

"I did not intend to climb trees as a career," Meg wrote years later in her book *Life in the Treetops*. "In fact, I tried desperately to think of alternatives to climbing—such as training a monkey, using large telephoto cameras on pulleys, or working along cliff edges where rain-forest treetops were at eye level."

Meg had had visions of sitting on a swing while she counted rain forest butterflies fluttering by. Instead, she had to learn how to climb trees far taller than any she had climbed before.

Members of a local spelunking (cave explorers) club kindly showed Meg how to use climbing gear to ascend and descend. Though this equipment was not easy to find in Australia, Meg managed to obtain one device for ascending called a jumar, another one for descending called a whale's tail, and specialized rope for climbers. Since she couldn't purchase a climbing harness, she fashioned one out of seatbelt straps. With this secured around her waist, she could attach herself to the rope for protection in case she fell.

Unlike rock climbing, where the climber finds handholds on rock faces, a tree climber must somehow loop her rope over a high limb and then use the jumar to slowly inch her way up. A slingshot works well for shooting a weight over a limb. Attached to the weight is fishing line that can be tied to cord that is connected to the end of a rope. First the fishing line is pulled over the limb, and then the cord is used to get the rope in place.

With practice, Meg was soon using the slingshot like a pro and had her first rope rigged. Next she had to master ascending with the jumar. At first she flailed and flipped upside down, but eventually she managed to stay upright and reach the treetops. As Meg used this method, called single-rope climbing, she enjoyed the feeling of rising into the high branches as much as she did when scrambling in the trees as a child.

Meg was now, along with other young scientists around the world, a pioneer of the treetops. Meg's mission in upper tree space was to keep track of thousands of individual leaves growing in the forest canopy in Mount Keira Preserve, just south of Sydney. She wanted to know what sorts of defenses the leaves of each different tree species had against the herbivores (plant-eating creatures) that live in the canopy.

Meg selected five different tree species to study. Each species had leaf characteristics that she thought might protect it. One had tough, leathery leaves, and another had leaves that were toxic. The leaves of the giant stinging tree were covered in stiff, sharp, flesh-tearing hairs as well as fine stinging hairs. Meg numbered hundreds of leaves using a waterproof pen and painstakingly recorded each one's location in her field journal. She included comments noting coloration, growth, damage, and when a leaf died. Each month she returned to her tress of study to collect more data.

"My notebooks are full of numbers," she told the Raleigh, North Carolina, *News and Observer*, "how many insects there are and how many are eating, dates of leafing activity or insect epidemics. Then we crunch the numbers when we get home. That's the boring side, all the data."

As she marked and measured the leaves of giant stinging trees, Meg's hands became red and swollen from contact with the toxic hairs. The only way to reach these leaves was by hanging from a nearby tree that didn't have noxious foliage. Though she found the stinging tree repulsive, she was surprised when her data revealed that its leaves were devoured more than those of any other trees in her study. She discovered the culprit was a voracious beetle, the only creature to have adapted to the nasty hairs.

Many leaf-eating herbivores were not easy to catch in the act of defoliating rain forest trees. Meg called these stealthy creatures UFOs: unidentified feeding organisms. It was only when she visited her study area at night that she discovered that many of them, mostly beetles, fed at night. One beetle she collected was the first of many new beetle species Meg would go on to discover. Beetles such as ladybugs, weevils, and fireflies belong to an order of insects called *Coleoptera*, which are the most diverse group of organisms on Earth. Currently it is estimated that one out of four living things on the planet is a beetle. As Meg and other canopy ecologists explored this new frontier, they unveiled an intricate ecosystem never before seen.

Meg's studies of marked leaves continued after she earned her doctoral degree, and her long-term observations showed that the leaves of some species of rain forest trees stay alive on the branches for up to 15 years, far longer than the 3 years most botanists had believed they lived.

Meg accepted a postdoctorate position in Australia's New England District working with zoologist Hal Heatwole. A mysterious condition called dieback was killing high numbers of eucalyptus trees. Hal and Meg's mission was to investigate the cause of this blight. This was a challenging task because sometimes plant diseases seemed to be the cause, but in other cases leaf-eating insects were likely culprits. Meg and Hal also thought that ranching and orchard practices might play a role.

During investigations on large sheep stations, Meg met many graziers (ranchers). One young man, Andrew Burgess, showed an interest in her investigation—and also made known his interest in her. Meg also felt attracted to him, and they began spending time together. When she was offered a job in Puerto Rico, she turned it down and accepted Andrew's proposal to marry and start a family. Within a year their son Edward was born. Three years later Meg gave birth to James.

As the mother of two small children, it was a struggle for Meg to continue her life as a scientist. With little support from Andrew, who expected her to be a full-time mother and ranch wife, Meg was distressed. The marriage slowly unraveled. When she was offered a teaching post at Williams College, Andrew refused to join her. After 10 years in Australia, Meg returned to America with Edward and James to begin the next chapter of her life.

Being a single mother, professor, and researcher was not easy, but Meg was happy. Anxious to teach her advanced ecology students about tree canopies, Meg partnered with an arborist from a nearby town to build a canopy walkway. Located in the Williams College research forest, it was the first of many walkways for which Meg oversaw construction throughout the United States and in other parts of the world. During her canopy investigations with students, they discovered that flying squirrels and white-footed mice living in the canopy were predators of gypsy moths and might be a key to controlling populations of this invasive moth. Fellow scientists came to visit her, and some urged her not to return to Australia.

In the early 1990s, the public was becoming aware of the rapid destruction of rain forests, and activists were demanding that this must stop. Scientists like Meg were revealing not only how many unknown plants and animals exist

Meg and her coworker D. C. on a canopy walkway.
Courtesy of Meg Lowman

in the forest canopy but also that many rain forest plants contain substances that might serve as future medicines. Canopy walkways were becoming tourist attractions in tropical communities where villagers saw a chance to earn income from tourism rather than logging.

Meg was invited to participate in a study with an international team of scientists that would investigate the forest canopy in the West African nation of Cameroon. Rather than ascending with ropes or constructing walkways, they would perch atop the canopy on an inflatable raft tethered to a hot-air balloon. "My childhood aspirations had come true. I traveled like Dorothy in *The Wizard of Oz!*" said Meg.

Next Meg sampled canopy leaves in Panama from a crane more than 10 stories high, and then in 1994 she was appointed chief scientist for the Jason Project, an investigation of tree crowns in Belize, Central America. She supervised the construction of a canopy walkway, which eight-year-old Eddie and six-year-old James dubbed their "giant tree house."

The goal of the Jason Project was to share the

Meg's sons, James and Edward, with a shaman in Belize.
Courtesy of Meg Lowman

process of scientific discoveries in remote locales via live satellite broadcasts to hundreds of thousands of students at schools, museums, and other educational centers all over the world. In her role Meg shared her passion for canopy research and her mission to protect rain forests.

As Edward and James grew into teens and then young men, Meg directed an expedition to the Peruvian Amazon to learn from a local shaman about medicinal rain forest plant products. She organized a volunteer group to assist villagers and priests in protecting the only remaining forests in Ethiopia. Over the years Meg continued her work as a researcher, educator, and promoter of forest conservation. Together with childhood best friend Betsy Hilfiger and her by-then-famous clothes designer brother, Tommy, they raised funds for Meg's Treetops Camp for disadvantaged girls in their hometown of Elmira.

Meg's wish is that some of the many people she has taught—the girls at her camp, visitors to the North Carolina Nature Research Center that Meg directs, or the numerous students in her classes—will spend their lives as scientists in the forest canopy or elsewhere, making discoveries about the world and learning how to preserve the rich diversity of life on Earth for future generations.

Pamela Rasmussen

BIRDING ACROSS CONTINENTS

> *"Pam would open the book and say, 'OK, which of the birds on this page do you like best?' Then she would do the same thing for the next page—all the way through the book."* —Sally Rasmussen, Pamela's sister

When Pamela Rasmussen was 10 years old, she discovered a wild diversity of birds through the pictures on the pages of a book given to her by her mother. Arthur Singer's illustrations in the junior edition of *Birds of the World* captivated her. As she flipped through the pages showing each bird in its varied habitat, from penguins to parrots, it was as if she were visiting them in their homes all over the world. In discovering these birds she had found a new world. She now dreamed of traveling all over the planet to see the birds pictured in the book.

Pamela Rasmussen was born on October 16, 1959, in Oregon, where her family lived in the small town of Hillsboro, 20 miles from Portland. In the Pacific Northwest, Pam could only imagine what it would be like to see exotic birds such as hornbills, toucans, and birds of paradise, but there were still local birds she could see. One day, she noticed a long-billed marsh wren singing in some rushes near her home. It was the first of many native birds Pam got to know. She was now so bird crazy that her idea of a perfect birthday was bird watching on the Oregon coast. Each October Pam, her sister, Sally, and their mom piled into the car for a drive to the seashore. No matter the weather, Pam was thrilled by each new species she saw. Sally, however, was not always enthusiastic.

"There we'd be freezing, looking for ducks," remembered Sally.

Helen Rasmussen was a single mom at this point, and she was devoted to her daughters. She drove Pam into the city to look at bird books in the Portland library. As a devout Seventh-Day Adventist, she felt it was her religious duty to shield Pam from scientific theories such as evolution that she believed contradicted the Christian bible. Each Saturday she took Sally and Pam to church. Unlikely as it may seem, Pam's relationship with the church ended up connecting her to future bird watching experiences.

In high school when she traveled with other Seventh-Day Adventists to perform a service project in Mexico, Pam finally got to see some of the exotic bird species pictured in *Birds of the World*, such as colorful tanagers and flashy hummingbirds. Following high school graduation she entered Walla Walla University, a Seventh-Day Adventist school, and the next summer she taught at a missionary school in Kenya. There she saw tropical birds, such as hoopoes, sunbirds, bee-eaters, black kites, and bulbuls. Back in Walla Walla, Pam read about an ornithologist who had recently discovered a new bird species in Peru and imagined herself finding new species of birds someday. Little did she know how important her future discoveries would be.

After receiving her bachelor's degree in science, Pam remained at Walla Walla College to earn a master's. Her chance to study birds in the field came in the summer of 1982 when she began research for her master's project on Protection Island National Wildlife Refuge off the northwest tip of Washington State. Spending day after day in the raucous nesting colony observing nestling pigeon guillemots was an entirely new experience. These small seabirds can dive more than 140 feet below the surface to catch small fish, crabs, and mollusks. They belong in a group of birds called alcids, which includes puffins, murres, razorbills, and auklets, but in some ways they are very different from their close relatives. Instead of feeding their nestlings at night like other alcids, pigeon guillemots provide meals to their little ones during the day. Although the other alcids lay only one egg, pigeon guillemots lay two. Pam took careful measurements of the guillemot nestlings during her two months on the island to find out how fast they grow.

Pam's study showed that pigeon guillemot nestlings develop more rapidly than those of other alcids, despite the fact that the adults must feed two chicks. Catching food during the day appeared to be a great advantage. One day during her research Pam noticed that one nestling had eaten its nest mate. Though cannibalism is common among hawks and owls, this was the first time the behavior had been observed in alcids. When Pam reported it in the *Wilson Bulletin*, it was the first of many articles she would publish in a scientific publication.

Having braved a summer in a nesting colony and earned her master's degree, she was now ready to further investigate the life of birds. The next step in Pam's education would be as a doctoral student at the University of Kansas, and her next field research would take place along the remote and rugged coasts of southern South America. Living along these coastlines are king and blue-eyed shags, also called cormorants, which are very similar in behavior and coloration. Pam wondered whether they were different species or merely varieties of the same species. To solve this mystery, she first examined shag skins in museum collections. Then in 1985, she traveled to the coasts of southern Chile, Argentina, and the Falkland Islands with her professor and a postdoctoral student. Her aim was to observe shags and collect specimens to make study skins.

The shags roosted along the rocky coasts that the researchers visited via a small inflatable boat. Pam was nervous every time a whale breached, sometimes only a few meters away, but she soon got used to them. Even in summer the weather in the region—close to Antarctica—is often wet, windy, and cold, which often made camping and fieldwork uncomfortable. Pam was frustrated that she did not speak Spanish, the language of both Chile and Argentina, and having to rise at dawn after eating dinner at the customary 10:00 PM left her exhausted. Overall she was happy to be observing shags in the beautiful landscape. Little by little, as she pieced together the relationship between the king and blue-eyed shag, Pam became confident that rather than being subspecies, they were actually forms of the same species, *Phalacrocorax atriceps*.

In 1992, with her PhD completed, Pam landed her dream job at the Smithsonian Institution working for S. Dillon Ripley. As head of the Smithsonian for 20 years he had overseen the incredible growth of its museums and publications. Dillon was also a legendary ornithologist. He was coauthor—with Salim Ali, the birdman of India—of a massive 10-volume book, *Birds of India*. Dillon was almost 80 years old, and his last ambition was to produce a field guide of the birds of South Asia. He hired Pam to assist him on this project. However, soon after Pam started this job, Dillon's health began to fail. He was seldom at work, leaving Pam without any supervision. She received some assistance from an ornithologist who had previously worked for Dillon.

Pam took on the task of completing the field guide with the same intensity she had as a child looking through *Birds of the World*. In a short time she had to become familiar with the 1,441 bird species found in India, Pakistan, Afghanistan, Bangladesh, Nepal, Bhutan, and the islands of Sri Lanka and the Maldives. To accomplish this, she examined thousands of bird skins at the Smithsonian, which houses the worlds largest avian collection (more than 600,000 specimens), as well as collections in New York and London. This was necessary to confirm which species would be included in the guide and where each had been seen. She corresponded and met with ornithologists from many South Asian nations, but best of all, she was able to travel in

South Asia to find, photograph, and record bird species, as well as collect needed specimens. "The job seemed like it was too good to be true," remembered Pam.

Pam pictured with bird skins at Michigan State University.
Courtesy of Pamela Rasmussen

With Dillon less and less involved in the project, Pam had to search for funding for her travels and find the time to contact government authorities about getting permits to do research. Her travel could take place during the summer while Dillon, who was from a wealthy family, vacationed at a large estate in Connecticut. Summer is monsoon season, a time of torrential rains in much of South Asia. Searching and collecting under such soggy conditions was not easy. On Pam's first trip to the Himalayas, leeches of all sizes rained down on her from trailside plants and latched onto whatever skin they could find. This would become a serious field hazard years later when Pam developed an allergic reaction to leeches and had to carry an EpiPen to slow the reaction until she could get medical care.

At the Smithsonian, her work was both challenging and rewarding. Pam's careful examination of museum specimens led to her discovering and describing four new species of Asian birds: three owls and a bush warbler. However, she was soon to make an even more startling discovery. In 1996 Pam read an article by an Irish ornithologist in which he claimed that two specimens of common redpolls in the collection of ornithologist Colonel Richard Meinertzhagen were fakes. Bird collectors have distinctive methods of preparing skins, and ornithologist Alan Knox had noticed that these two bird skins, which Meinertzhagen noted as coming from France, were prepared using techniques identical to redpolls prepared by another collector in Great Britain almost 70 years before the date listed on one of Meinertzhagen's redpoll specimens. Pam was alarmed. She knew how much S. Dillon Ripley and Salim Ali had relied on Meinertzhagen's collection for research. Pam decided to investigate.

"I thought to myself, if he went to the trouble to steal and change the data on a common bird like a redpoll, wouldn't he also try to fake some of the rarer birds?" Pam Rasmussen recounted later to a journalist.

Pam flew to Great Britain to work with Robert Pry-Jones, head of the British Natural History Museum's bird group. Pam hoped Alan was wrong, but she and Robert soon uncovered a massive fraud. Meinertzhagen had not only collected an extraordinary number of bird specimens, he had also stolen many specimens from collections made by other scientists. He then relabeled them, listing himself as the collector, and invented fictitious locations and dates. In the case of one bird, the forest owlet, the false labeling had prevented Dillon and other ornithologists from finding it in the wild. Because Meinertzhagen sometimes tinkered with the stolen specimens to hide the style of the original maker, Pam decided to investigate further. The forest owlet had not been seen since 1914, when Meinertzhagen had supposedly collected it. With help from colleagues and the FBI lab, she proved the specimen in the Meinertzhagen collection had materials identical to the forest owlet skins collected by James Davidson in 1884. Now Pam knew where to find the missing owlet. The actual collection site was about 300 miles from where Meinertzhagen had falsely claimed he had collected it. In 1997 she went on an expedition with Ben King of the American Museum of Natural History to the site where Davidson had collected his owlets in 1884. To their dismay they found that most of the forest had been logged. On their last day of searching, they were about to give up, thinking the owlet must now be extinct. Suddenly King sighted a small owl up in a tree, and Pam confirmed that it was indeed a forest owlet.

"You can imagine the thrill when we realized what we were seeing! But my first thought would be better described as terror, because [at] any moment I fully expected the bird to fly off," Pam said in an interview. Fortunately, it perched long enough for Pam to record the sighting on video.

Pam recording bird vocalizations in India.
Nikhil Devasar

In 1997 Pam, John Rappole of the National Geographic Society, and German ornithologist Swen Renner became some of the first Western scientists allowed to visit Myanmar (previously known as Burma), a country that had been ruled for years by a brutal military dictatorship. Pam later returned to Myanmar for more expeditions to collect data on the effects of climate change and to census the bird species of this little-known region. On the first trip her seemingly romantic transport on an elephant was so bouncy that she found it was more pleasant and just as fast to walk. On the second trip her gear ended up in the wrong location, a zone that the army had barred to foreign visitors. She and her Burmese colleagues had to sneak in, grab the gear, and then quickly travel to their study site. Pam's 2006 expedition with John Rappole and Burmese conservationist Thein Aung was during the monsoon season in June and July, when birds are nesting. By capturing birds in special nets called mist nets and conducting both visual and auditory surveys, they confirmed the presence of 137 species, some previously unknown in the area.

In 2005, after almost 15 years of work, *Birds of South Asia: The Ripley Guide* was finally published—but to Pam it seemed her work had only begun. Her keen attention to detail and her vast knowledge of the birds of South Asia enabled her to confirm discoveries of new birds. Two of these were new Philippine owl species whose songs she recorded in 2012.

"When we first heard the songs, we were amazed because they were so distinctly different that we realized they were new species," Pam later reported. These recordings, produced by Pam and other ornithologists, became available to the public through one of her most ambitious projects—AVoCet (Avian Vocalizations Center). Pam started this project with the hope that one day it would contain recordings of all the Earth's bird species.

Being a major force in discovering what bird species exist on the planet and working to protect them takes persistence and dedication. Pam is grateful to have a supportive husband, paleo-biologist Michael Gottfried, as well as students and other scientists to collaborate with. Her life as an ornithologist, museum curator, and professor is busy and incredibly rewarding. For Pamela Rasmussen, who dreamed of a life spent learning about birds, it couldn't be much better. Each year there are new birds to see and record, new questions to pursue, and new discoveries to make.

Kate Jackson

IN QUEST OF SCALY, SLIMY CREATURES

> *"It is just in my character to be brave and reckless."*
>
> —*Kate Jackson*

One day when Kate Jackson was five years old, her little sister unknowingly scooped a small water snake out of Lake Ontario and dumped it onto Kate's legs. It was the first live snake she had ever seen, and Kate screamed.

"Our sensible babysitter scolded me for making such a ridiculous fuss—a big girl like me!" remembered Kate in her book *Mean and Lowly Things*.

The babysitter's words made sense to her, and thus began her interest in slimy and scaly creatures. First it was frogs that grabbed her attention. She not only played with them, but she also pretended to be the "Frog Queen." As Kate pored over pictures of all the frog species in the *Peterson Field Guide of North American Reptiles and Amphibians*, she gradually learned their names. Next she did the same with the pictures of toads, then salamanders, as well as snakes and other reptiles.

Kate Jackson,
the Frog Queen.
Courtesy of Heather Jackson

Kate was born in Toronto, Canada, on February 14, 1972. Her father often took Kate and her sister to explore at a ravine near her family's house. One day they found some toad tadpoles and brought them home in a jar of pond water. With their father's help, the girls converted an old baby bathtub into a toad pond. As the tadpoles developed into adult toads, the girls observed each stage with fascination.

At age 12 Kate babysat the children of her parents' friends. The father was a professor who studied sea turtles, and he encouraged Kate's interest in herpetology, the study of reptiles and amphibians. He brought her to a Herpetological Society meeting, where he introduced Kate to adults who shared her passion. At another meeting, when Kate was 13 years old, she volunteered to be its secretary when no one else showed interest. Kate's mother became fond of saying that she had never known what a herpetologist was until she gave birth to one.

During a high school career day, Kate spent time with the curator of herpetology at the Royal Ontario Museum. He showed her reptile and amphibian specimens carefully preserved in jars. For Kate, the most interesting were the forest cobra and a giant salamander, also called a hellbender. Each specimen was labeled with the species name, collector's name, and the collection location and date. What was even better for Kate than seeing specimens was learning how to prepare skeletons of dead specimens donated from zoos. She set to work on a monitor lizard, cobra, and small crocodile. It was so fascinating that the rest of the day flew by.

After high school Kate first attended Dalhousie University in Nova Scotia, where she took a part-time job as the tadpole caretaker in a lab examining the effects of zero gravity on animals. The next year she transferred to the University of Toronto to study herpetology. During the next few years Kate learned as much, if not more, about reptiles and amphibians from her jobs and internships as she learned in her courses.

Kate with a northern water snake, the species that started it all.
Courtesy of Kate Jackson

One summer Kate worked at a reptile-breeding center in Picton, two and a half hours east of Toronto. With training from Tom Mason, a zookeeper at the Toronto Zoo, she confidently took on the responsibility of caring for 70 reptiles. She rode to Picton each week, stayed in a rented room, and on the return trip with Tom often stopped to search for turtles, frogs, and snakes in swamps and ponds. On these informal expeditions Kate developed new skills as a field herpetologist.

Later that summer Kate managed the reptile-breeding center with two high school students and a pair of convicts in a work-release program as her helpers. During the following years Kate interned at an iguana farm in Costa Rica, worked for a summer at the Toronto Zoo, and was an intern at the herpetology department at the Smithsonian Institution in Washington, DC. Here she learned how to operate an electron microscope, which she used to examine snake fangs.

Kate graduated with honors in 1994. Before starting her master's studies, she accepted an opportunity to volunteer at a crocodile farm in Singapore. Mr. Lee, the farm's owner, had two daughters, Pei Hui and Pei Lin. The girls and Kate quickly become good friends. Before flying home Mr. Lee gave Kate six baby crocodiles packed in a Styrofoam box; they would be used for her master's research at the University of Toronto. At the Singapore airport an airline official refused to let Kate carry the baby crocs onboard her flight. Pei Hui and Pei Win and their friends came to the rescue by badgering the official so much that he relented.

Back in Toronto Kate studied the unusual sense organs found on crocodile skin, and after earning her master's degree, she enrolled in the doctoral program at Harvard University. Her adviser was curator and professor Dr. John Cadle, who had a reputation as an adventurous field scientist. As a lone explorer he had been struck by lightning as he searched for snakes in Madagascar. In Peru a leech crawled up his nose while he slept.

"He was the kind of herpetologist I wanted to be," remembered Kate.

In 1997, with one year at Harvard complete, Kate set off for another internship with the Smithsonian Institution, this time studying brown tree snakes on the Pacific island of Guam. By the next summer Kate was more than ready to organize her own research trip. The big question was, where should she go? Soon she became aware of the Congo, a country in Central Africa. "It was a virtual blank spot on the herpetological map of the world," wrote Kate.

Here she hoped to make new discoveries about the diversity of the reptiles and amphibians of Central Africa as well as aid in the effort to protect those that were endangered. Her only fear was of being bit by a venomous snake. She was terrified at making the mistake of confusing a venomous with a harmless species, not only because of the possibility of dying, but also that her thesis advisor would find out that she had made a mistake in identification. With a healthy mix of innocence and courage, Kate traveled alone to a country where she knew virtually nothing about its culture, politics, or how to successfully collect specimens in the tropics.

From the minute she arrived in Brazzaville, the Congo's largest city, Kate had her share of adventures. She had barely departed for the northern Congo to begin her search for reptiles and amphibians when a civil war erupted in the south. The pygmy guides she had hired at her research site became wary of her. While collecting a harmless house snake, she was bitten. The guides, who thought the snake was venomous, believed she was a witch because she survived the bite. But with their help her collection steadily grew—until one night when she tripped over a log and scraped her leg. The leg became infected, and nothing in her first aid kit helped cure it. Soon the infection was so bad that Kate feared she could lose her leg without medical attention. She was evacuated to a hospital in the neighboring nation of Cameroon; after she recovered she flew home.

Despite the abrupt end to Kate's expedition, she was able to collect and observe 20 amphibian and 17 reptile species. Of these, seven were species that had never before been collected in the Republic of Congo. When Kate was awarded the prestigious Women of Discovery Award (in the category of courage) given by Wings WorldQuest fourteen years later, her father joked to his friends, "Kate isn't brave; she is reckless."

Reckless or not, after this first expedition in the Congo, Kate was ready for more exploring.

Kate carefully catches a rattlesnake with her class.
Courtesy of Kate Jackson

Kate's doctoral research focused on the evolution of the venom-releasing organs and structures of venomous snakes. Her study revealed that snakes began evolving venom-releasing organs as long as 10 to 25 million years ago and that some species of harmless snakes evolved from venomous ancestors. For her work Kate was awarded her PhD in 2002, becoming Dr. Kate Jackson.

In 2005 she asked the curator of herpetology at the Smithsonian for funds to conduct an independent expedition to the Congo. Her plan was to collect the snakes and other "herps" in the flooded forests in the northern Congo for the Smithsonian collection. She was awarded barely enough money for her expedition but decided to go anyway.

From the start it was a challenging undertaking. After she arrived in Brazzaville, Kate's first obstacle was an interminably long delay in being granted a permit to collect specimens in the preserves she had arranged to survey. As she saw her time for her expedition fading away, she decided to revise her plan and collect in a part of the forest outside the preserve's boundary. Because this forest was under the jurisdiction of a small village named Ganganya, she had to get permission from the village leaders and pay them a fee.

Without the use of the lodging at the preserve, Kate had to hire a cook and a guide. With their help she set up a camp on the edge of the flooded forest. Life was not easy there; she endured torrential rains, stinging ants, biting flies, and unappetizing meals. Despite setting up nets and pitfall traps as well as training her guide, Etienne, and cook, Florence, to help her collect, Kate didn't find as many specimens as she had hoped. Finally, by setting out more nets and encouraging villagers to bring her reptiles and amphibians, Kate was able to expand her collection. A little boy brought her a species of African clawed frog she hadn't seen before. A local Pygmy man, Fiti, brought her other uncommon frog species and snakes.

One day they caught a six-foot-long water cobra in one of the nets. This venomous snake was too big for any of their bags, so Kate had to put it in her day pack. Kate's clothes were constantly wet from incessant rains and the daily wading necessary to check the nets. Toward the end of her expedition her guide and cook became more and more unreliable. Food began to run low, as well as the lab supplies she needed for preserving specimens. Despite these difficulties, Kate collected 130 specimens. She also photographed many of them while they were still alive and was the first scientist to procure tissue samples of Congolese species for later DNA analysis. It was both an exhilarating and exhausting experience.

When Kate arrived at the airport for the flight home, the airlines refused to transport her collection. As Kate flew off without her hard-earned specimens, tears rolled down her cheeks. Fortunately, a local French scientist took charge of her collection and later shipped it to the Smithsonian. Kate was slim when she left for the Congo, but when she returned to Toronto 10 pounds lighter, she was practically a skeleton. But despite all of the difficulties she experienced, Kate began making arrangements for another expedition to the Congo in November and December 2006.

This time, Kate experienced her worst fear. One day while collecting from a village brick pile she mistook a partially visible forest cobra for a nonvenomous species. Before she was able to drop it in her snake bag, she received a small prick from its fangs. She didn't know how deep the bite was, but snake venom was running all down her arm. Being surrounded by village children, who had been helping her remove the bricks, meant she was unable to just drop the cobra. Soon her hands started to go numb. Once the snake was safely in the bag, Kate rushed back to camp. There she instructed her assistant, Ange, to inject snake antivenom into her abdomen. Fortunately Kate survived the incident without any permanent injury. It was a scary and humbling experience. From then on Kate would use more caution as she collected venomous snakes.

Kate remembered these trips for their hardships, dangers, and loneliness but also for her new friendships and the kindness shown to her, even though some considered her a sorcerer. At the end of this trip Kate entered a new stage in her life by accepting an assistant teaching job at Whitman College in Washington State. In 2010 she published her well-acclaimed book *Mean and Lowly Things: Snakes, Science, and Survival in the Congo*. In 2012 she and her partner, Andrea, became the mothers of a little boy.

Will Kate now, like her mother, raise a young herpetologist? Only time will tell. Meanwhile Kate is a nurturing mother, an inspiring teacher, and an occasionally reckless explorer.

Professor Kate Jackson plays Medusa with some garter snakes.
Courtesy of Kate Jackson

Aparajita Datta

VANISHING WILDLIFE AND FORGOTTEN PEOPLE

> *"We are up at four in the morning, slogging our way through mud and slush in landslide-prone terrain, walking 12 hours a day through thick vegetation and rivers. The Lisu people are right by our side. They've shown and told me things I would never otherwise have known." —Aparajita Datta*

Torrential rains frequently occur in the mountains of Himachal Pradesh, one of India's northernmost states. After one such storm, Aparajita Datta became one of many people stranded in a small mountain lodge when the rains washed out the road. The only route they could take to the nearest village was a 50-mile trek through mountainous terrain. This journey was so rugged that some of the people whom Aparajita walked with died along the way.

Aparajita Datta was born in Calcutta, India, on January 5, 1970. During her early years in India she was fascinated by the natural world, particularly animals. She loved dogs as well as other pets and dreamed of being a veterinarian. In 1978, her father,

Aparajita Datta.
Courtesy of Aparajita Datta

who worked as an accountant, accepted a job in Zambia, Africa. Her family then moved to Lusaka, the nation's capital. This small city felt like a village compared to Calcutta, which had a population 18 times larger. While Aparajita attended the International School of Lusaka, her American teacher noticed Aparajita's interest in nature and gave her special attention. Her teacher hosted an after-school zoo/science club in which Aparajita and other students observed and cared for chameleons and other creatures. They also "adopted" and chose the name for a cheetah housed at the Lusaka zoo, which they occasionally went to see. Aparajita's favorite books were about animals, and she especially enjoyed animal encyclopedias.

Southern Africa teemed with wildlife. Aparajita wanted to explore outdoors, but her father worried about her safety and didn't let her roam far from home. For Aparajita, it was especially thrilling to see lions, elephants, giraffes, and hippos in the wild. On vacations she; her younger brother, Arijit; and her parents would visit not only Zambia's South Luangwa National Park, but also game parks in bordering countries. On one trip to Luangwa Valley, she pleaded with her parents for permission to go on a night safari accompanied by other lodge guests. Her father refused to let her go off with strangers. The following day Aparajita was deeply disappointed after hearing that a rhino and a serval cat had been sighted. When Aparajita learned about the wildlife biologists who worked in the parks, she wanted to become one herself.

After five years in Zambia, she returned to Calcutta to live with her grandparents and attend school. She missed Africa and her old school. In India learning was more regimented and competitive. It was a struggle to keep up in her math classes, which were at a more advanced level than those she had taken in Lusaka. She had to take classes in Hindi, India's official language, as well as Bengali, the language of Bengal, where Calcutta is located. She did not like the rote teaching style in which teachers lectured and students were expected to memorize mountains of facts just to perform well on tests. Because Aparajita was both bright and adaptable, she soon caught up in math. She made friends who shared her interests, and best of all she had an inspiring biology teacher, Mrs. De, who took Aparajita under her wing.

Though her parents wished for Aparajita to pursue a professional career, such as law or medicine, they allowed her to study botany at Calcutta's Presidency College. Uninspired by her courses, she spent most of her time loafing about in the canteen instead of studying, and her poor grades showed it. Ultimately, after graduation Aparajita found the right program for the next stage of her schooling.

"I finally translated my dreams of studying ecology into reality by joining the Wildlife Institute of India, Dehradun, for a master's degree in wildlife ecology," Aparajita later wrote.

Located in the foothills of the Himalayas in India's northernmost region, the institute was close to the southern forests of Dehradun and not far from wildlife preserves and national parks. There were only six other students in her group and only one other woman among them. One student was a young man from Delhi named Charudutt Mishra. Like Aparajita, he had been fascinated with animals and nature since childhood. She and Charu soon fell in love.

For her master's project Aparajita studied the food-gathering patterns of Indian giant squirrels. These mega-rodents are as long from head to tail as foxes and are champion jumpers that can leap as far as 20 feet from one tree to another. To study them she had to follow their daily schedule. This meant getting up early enough every morning to be at her study site at dawn and returning to the site again every evening at dusk. Aparajita learned how to be stealthy enough not to scare off the squirrels as they foraged in the treetops. With days and days of practice, she became a skilled observer and detailed note taker.

After completing her thesis in 1993, Aparajita worked at a series of jobs, beginning with three months of trapping and

Aparajita at ease in the forest.
Courtesy of Aparajita Datta

tracking wolves. This was followed by an investigation of the impact of logging in the forests of Arunachal Pradesh on the lives of squirrels and tree-dwelling primates, such as monkeys. This region, with its rich biological and cultural diversity, fascinated Aparajita. Her next job was in an extremely different landscape high in the lofty land of Ladakh in the Kashmir region of northwestern India. In this land of stunted plants, she studied the social behavior of Himalayan marmots, a cousin of groundhogs that live in colonies.

All these field experiences prepared Aparajita for the final step in her education, earning a PhD in science. In 1996, Charu left for Amsterdam to start his doctoral studies, and the next year Aparajita started her doctoral studies at Saurashtra University in Rajkot. This city lies near India's eastern coast not far from the border with Pakistan. However, Aparajita's doctoral study would take place back in her beloved Arunachal Pradesh. There she planned to investigate the ecology of hornbills in Pakke Wildlife Sanctuary. Aparajita wondered how important wreathed and great hornbills were in dispersing seeds throughout tropical forests. Hornbills are named for their extremely large curved bills. With their long wings they can easily travel from one area of the forest to another. Aparajita already knew that hornbills were found in recently logged areas and the second-growth forests that grow up after logging. What she wondered was if the birds living in old-growth forests were important for the forests' long-term survival.

One morning she set out to count the number of figs a male hornbill would eat per minute. "No time for tea, so I pull on clothes and leech-proof socks and walk rapidly down the trail to a ficus tree laden with ripe, black-red figs. I might well have gone alone in the cold December dawn; the tree is not far from camp. But Japang Pansa, my Wancho field assistant, accompanies me, as I do not fancy an encounter on my own with elephants in the feeble light," Aparajita wrote.

Aparajita spotted a hornbill and started observing. After he flew away she and Japang examined the area beneath the tree where the male hornbill and his mate had dropped figs. Here she found recently regurgitated seeds from fruits other than figs. These were some of the first clues to discovering how far the hornbills flew to the other area to eat. Over the next few years, Aparajita accumulated more and more evidence of where hornbills foraged. In her PhD thesis she revealed that hornbills disperse the seeds of more than 80 rainforest tree species, some of which rely entirely on hornbills to spread and plant their seeds. That was why Aparajita dubbed hornbills "the farmers of the forest."

Aparajita and Charu were married in 1999, but that didn't mean they could spend much time together. Though Charu's

Great hornbill.
Courtesy of Wikimedia Commons

fieldwork was in India, his area of study was far to the north, high up in the Himalayan Mountains. There he investigated how the survival of wild bharal, also known as Himalayan blue sheep, was affected by the grazing of domestic livestock such as yak and horses. Aparajita was working many miles south and thousands of feet lower in the humid tropical forests.

As Aparajita got better acquainted with the local tribal people, such as the Lisu, Nishi, Tangsa, and Singpho, she learned more about their history, culture, and daily lives. She was shown the beautiful ornaments they made out of the bills and feathers of hornbills. As an ecologist this bothered her. As a fellow human she knew that people have traditionally hunted animals for food and other uses. What concerned her was that creatures such as hornbills were becoming scarcer as a result of logging. Due to this loss of forests Japang Pansa and his people had fewer places to hunt and grow food. To Aparajita it was obvious that protecting old-growth forests in more national parks, such as Pakke or Namdapha, was not the solution. The creation of parks forced tribal people off their lands and still didn't solve the problem of wildlife being killed by poaching. Aparajita believed there must be another approach but wasn't yet sure what it was.

After completing her PhD program, Aparajita moved to Mysore to work with both the Nature Conservation Foundation and the Wildlife Conservation Society-India Program. In 2002 she conducted a survey in eastern Arunachal to examine the connection between the hornbill population status and the hunting practices of tribal communities. Her developing relationship with these hunters led to the discovery of two species of muntjac, the leaf deer and black barking deer, neither of which had been known to occur in India.

The next year she joined up with Charu and their colleague M. D. Madhusudan on an expedition to the secluded, high-altitude zone of the eastern Himalayas in Arunachal Pradesh. Their sighting of a Chinese goral, a small goatlike animal, was the first record of its presence in India. The biggest discovery of the trip, however, was finding a macaque species new to science. This large old-world monkey with a short tail and dark face was later named the Arunachal macaque. It is unique in being one of the only primate species to live above 11,000 feet. These discoveries led to the establishment of the first high-altitude wildlife reserve in the region.

Aparajita eventually returned to Arunachal to conduct more studies of hornbills and to take a census of populations of large mammals, such as sun bears, tigers, clouded leopards, and musk deer in Namdapha National Park. This was pioneering work because more than 90 percent of the park's territory was still unexplored by scientists. To assist her in finding and monitoring hornbills, she hired three former Lisu hunters. While out in the field with them, Aparajita was amazed by how easily they traveled through rugged hills on the faint trails. As she became more aware of their deep knowledge of the park's flora and fauna, she gained a whole new perspective. Aparajita now realized that their in-depth understanding could be used to manage the park. This challenged her notion of the problem being conservationists versus hunters.

"It is impossible to convince tribal people to be part of wildlife conservation without first understanding and having empathy for their own fundamental needs," Aparajita Datta explained in an interview with the National Geographic Society.

By 2003 Aparajita was ready to try to put some of her new ideas into practice by initiating a community-based conservation program. As she trained more tribal hunters to help her track down, monitor, and protect wildlife, she learned not only how much they knew about forest animals but also how much they cared about them. One ex-hunter she hired to help her locate hornbill nests, a Nishi tribesman named Taya Tayum, proudly informed her he had killed at least 30 hornbills. He also told her about carrying a sick hornbill 12 miles to a vet, in hope that it could be saved. Without being able to hunt, she knew that local people would need another source of food and income.

Aparajita found the funds to provide medical support and health care training for tribal communities. She helped establish kindergartens and teacher training programs for teens. With money earned from working as field assistants and wildlife protectors, Nishi hunters had less need to hunt. Within three years the numbers of animals hunted steadily declined.

"The only way Namdapha can survive in the future is if the Lisu and other tribal groups (like the Tangsa and Singpho) are brought in as its main protector. Instead of treating the Lisu as enemies, Namdapha should be protected by the community that knows the most about it," Aparajita wrote in a 2005 article.

On various excursions with her conservation partners, Aparajita has been led on trails to remote areas where she has often crossed rickety bamboo bridges suspended over rushing streams. On one occasion elephants charged her, and another time she was almost swept away while crossing a raging creek. When she was badly stung by wasps, she had to continue trekking for several more days with her face grotesquely swollen before she could get medical help. When she came face-to-face with a tiger, her curiosity was greater than her fear, and she didn't panic. As a woman who works alone in remote places, Aparajita is on her guard not only for wild creatures such as tigers or elephants. Once, a man attempted to break into her room at a rest house and the drunken caretaker didn't hear her plea for help, so Aparajita slept for the remainder of the night with her knife in her hand.

Aparajita dressed for work wearing her pack and gaiters. *Courtesy of Aparajita Datta*

Unlike her childhood years, when her chances to explore were limited, as an adult Aparajita has had many opportunities to visit places few scientists have ever been. Like most field biologists, Aparajita takes discomforts in stride, especially if it means being able see the world through the eyes of people such as the Nishi and Lisu. "Often, an entire day's walk using 'shortcuts' that Lisus love to take will involve several river crossings, wading through slush, walking for hours over slippery rocks along shadowy streams, vaulting over bamboo thickets and thorny cane and countless ups and downs," Aparajita recounted.

In 2004 Aparajita and Charu received the Earth Heroes Award given by India's *Sanctuary Asia* magazine. In 2009 Wings WorldQuest gave Aparajita the Women of Discovery Humanity Award for her community-based conservation efforts. The next year she was one of 14 people selected to be a National Geographic Emerging Explorer. The best award, however, was the birth of her and Charu's son, Shivi. Imagine having a mother whose advice to all of us is, "Don't ever lose your curiosity or sense of wonder."

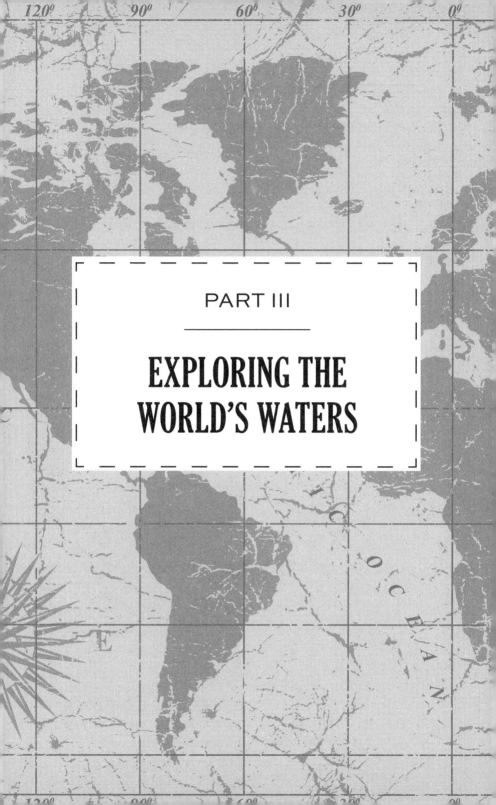

PART III

EXPLORING THE WORLD'S WATERS

Eleanor Creesy

SHE SETS THE COURSE

> *"[Eleanor Creesy's] skills are considered to be a major factor in the ship's safe and swift passages."* —Daily Alta California, *April 20, 1854*

On April 15, 1851, the clipper ship *Flying Cloud* slid down the rails from Donald McKay's shipyard and splashed into Boston Harbor. Like other clippers, its bow was as streamlined as the head of a codfish, and its stern was as trim as a mackerel's tail. It was an astonishing 235 feet long, 41 feet wide, and weighed 1,782 tons. The main mast towered 127 feet above the deck. As the biggest ship in the harbor, it was indeed a spectacular sight to behold.

In less than two months *Flying Cloud* would set sail on its maiden voyage from New York to San Francisco, but first the ship had be towed to New York Harbor. There it would be loaded with cargo and provisions for the long voyage to the Golden State.

As the ship was pulled away from shore, Eleanor Creesy, the ship's navigator, lined up the needle of her compass with the

Boston lighthouse to determine the magnetic bearing. She plotted a line of position on her nautical chart, starting at the lighthouse and running seaward.

Eleanor was used to calculating the location of her ship and setting the best course for it to follow. For the past 10 years, since the age of 26, she had journeyed across the seas with her husband, Captain Josiah Perkins Creesy. They had just returned from Shanghai, China, on the *Oneida*, a ship that had been their main home for the past five years. Now Josiah was the captain of *Flying Cloud*, a vessel that he and the ship's owners hoped would be the fastest of the new clipper ships.

Eleanor was born on September 21, 1814, in Marblehead, Massachusetts, a seafaring village north of Boston. She was the only child of Mary and John Prentiss until her younger sister was born when Eleanor was in her 20s. John Prentiss was the well-respected schooner captain of a vessel named the *Californian*. When he started teaching young Eleanor how to navigate a ship, he had no notion that one day she would pilot vessels to California and other faraway places.

The townsfolk gossiped when Captain Prentiss instructed his daughter in the basics of navigation. They couldn't understand why he was teaching Eleanor a skill that was practiced solely by men. In the 1820s very few girls attended school, and if they did, one of the few career options open to them was teaching. But Captain Prentiss loved navigation, and since he didn't have a son as an apprentice, he saw no reason not to pass his knowledge on to his clever and interested daughter.

For Eleanor, it was a welcome challenge for her bright mind. With an aptitude for math, she quickly grasped the geometry skills necessary to execute navigational computations. She was thrilled to learn how to use navigation instruments such as a sextant and compass. A sextant determines a ship's location in the ocean through taking readings of the position of the sun, moon, and certain stars. Eleanor practiced and practiced using these tools. She repeated complex calculations until she had finally mastered the basic skills of navigating a ship. Captain Prentiss beamed with pride for his smart and hardworking student.

In Marblehead most young women looked forward to marrying a sailor and taking care of a home and children. Eleanor's girlfriends couldn't understand why she wanted to learn the skills of navigating a ship. They couldn't even imagine that she might actually one day serve as a ship's navigator, because they had never heard of a woman doing such a thing. For Eleanor, navigation was not only a joy but also a path to a bigger life than that available to a Marblehead wife. She had no desire to stay home while her husband roamed the high seas. She wished for a life at sea and hoped her training in navigation would earn her a place aboard a ship. Being beautiful and from a good family, Eleanor had many suitors, but she turned them all away. She patiently waited for the right man, one who would respect her for her intelligence and would support her goal of serving as a ship's navigator.

Finally, at the age of 26, she met that man. Captain Josiah Perkins Creesy was only six months older than Eleanor but had already been a captain for three years. Perkins, as she called him, was attracted by Eleanor's fine looks and sharp mind and was happily surprised by her navigational skills. She was definitely not the kind of wife he had expected to find in Marblehead. It was not uncommon for a captain's wife to travel with her husband on voyages. Many served as the ship's nurse. Some even gave birth aboard their husband's ship. Eleanor and Perkins's marriage, however, was a partnership both in love and occupation. She plotted the courses for Perkins's ships, nursed passengers and crew, and organized the provisioning of all the food required to feed more than five dozen people for many months at sea. Not only was Captain Creesy's wife unusual in being a navigator, but she would also prove to be one of the most capable navigators of their time.

During her first 10 years of sailing with her husband, Eleanor navigated on numerous journeys to China, during which she gained a familiarity with the world's oceans. Despite their extensive time at sea, neither she nor Perkins had ever rounded Cape Horn at the southern tip of South America, and never before had they had so much pressure to perform their duties. The owners of their new ship, the *Flying Cloud*, hoped that it would be the fastest clipper ship yet built. On May 24, as the *Flying Cloud* was readied in New York Harbor for its maiden voyage, another clipper, the *Challenge*, was launched from a New York shipyard. The *Challenge* was larger than the *Flying Cloud*, and its builder boasted that it would beat the *Flying Cloud* for the title of the fastest clipper ship of all time. Neither ship had been taken for a trial run before embarking on the 14,000-mile journey to San Francisco. Bets were made over which ship would reach California in the shortest time.

The *Flying Cloud* had so much room in its hold for goods and provisions that it took six weeks to load all the cargo, which included everything from mining equipment to bales of cotton and sacks of candles, soap, apples, and rice. There were casks of flour and wine; crates of tools, shoes, and boots; and even tubs of butter. Meanwhile, Perkins searched the waterfront of New York for experienced seamen and found 59, including a Chinese cook named Ching, to serve on his ship.

With its narrow, cleaver-like bow, the *Flying Cloud* was designed to slice swiftly through the sea. Its three masts held 21 large sails, amounting to 10,000 yards of sailcloth. This vast amount of sail would surely catch more wind than any previously built ship, but Perkins wondered how the masts would hold up to heavy gusts during a storm.

Eleanor spent the last nights of May studying the latest wind and current charts compiled by Lieutenant Matthew Fontaine Maury of the US Navy, based on information from thousands of voyages. Not all navigators intended to use this new information, but Eleanor knew the charts would be invaluable.

Finally, on June 2, 1851, the *Flying Cloud* set sail from New York Harbor.

"The beautiful vessel, almost hid by the cloud of canvas which she spread, seemed to glide through the waters as smoothly as a reindeer," the *New York Tribune* reported.

The *Flying Cloud* may have started off gliding, but within four days, on June 6, Eleanor calculated that the ship was racing through the sea. She determined it had sailed 280 miles in one 24-hour period. This meant it was traveling at a speed of 12.5 knots, far faster than most ships then sailing the seas.

That evening, just as dinner was about to be served, a loud crash shook the ship. The topmost part of the mainmast had broken off, taking with it the top of the mizzenmast. This hazardous tangle of splintered masts, spars, stays, and rigging swayed 100 feet above the deck. With every roll of the vessel, it pounded the lower part of the mainmast. Perkins was worried that the mast wouldn't be able to withstand much more battering before it, too, broke apart. Despite the risk, he had no choice but to order his sailors to climb up into the rigging and lower the broken pieces to the deck for repair.

Despite being tossed about, the sailors hung on tightly and skillfully lowered the debris, piece by piece, onto the deck. It took two full days for the ship's sailmaker and his assistant to repair the torn sails and for the crew to temporarily fix the mast and rigging. With great relief Perkins and Eleanor set the *Flying*

Cloud sailing once more, but they were concerned about how long the repairs would hold the mast together.

Three days later, on June 11, Eleanor changed the ship's course to follow a new one, based on advice from Lieutenant Maury. Instead of continuing east as most ships were, she guided *Flying Cloud* south in an attempt to cross a narrower part of the Doldrums. Sailing ships can be stranded for days or weeks in this windless region between the belt of trade winds to the north and the belt to the south near the equator around the globe. Even though Perkins was not as well versed in Maury's studies of wind and ocean currents, he trusted Eleanor to use her knowledge and intuition to adjust their course. Three days later, as they passed through the Doldrums in record time, they knew this route was far better than the old one. Soon they crossed the equator and were 3,780 miles from New York, breaking previous speed records. "We have passed the equator in two days less time than ever before," Captain Creesy recorded in his log.

The next two weeks were not smooth sailing for Perkins and Eleanor. For several days fierce gusts buffeted the *Flying Cloud*, straining the damaged mainmast. Eleanor nursed a passenger who had attempted suicide, and Perkins was forced to shackle two disgruntled sailors who had been caught attempting to damage the ship's cargo.

As they approached the Strait of Le Maire at the eastern tip of South America, more storms set in. All stove fires, lanterns, and candles were extinguished to prevent a fire from occurring onboard the ship as it rocked in the heavy seas, and because of this the temperature inside the cabins plunged to near freezing. Storm clouds blocked the sun in the day and stars at night, preventing Eleanor from using her sextant to determine the ship's exact location. Instead she had to make an educated guess, or dead reckoning, to estimate their position.

At times like this, only the skills of an experienced navigator could keep a ship from running ashore or veering far off course. When the storm finally ended two days later, Eleanor was pleased to discover that she had set the best course, and they were in the right place to enter the straits. After they were through the passage, Perkins and Eleanor steered the *Flying Cloud* on a safer, faster route around Cape Horn without any serious trouble. With all the sails set, they sped up the Pacific Coast of Chile toward California. In one day they covered 374 miles, which Eleanor calculated was the fastest a clipper had ever sailed.

Five days later they crossed the equator, made good time through another section of the Doldrums, and then for the next two weeks roared north powered by strong winds. On the last day of August they finally arrived in San Francisco. Their voyage of 89 days and 21 hours had set a new speed record, beating the previous record by an entire week. Perkins and Eleanor Creesy and the *Flying Cloud* were instantly famous in San Francisco.

An artist's rendering shows the *Flying Cloud* at sea with full sail.
Courtesy of Wikimedia Commons

Their accomplishment was seen as yet one more example of Yankee daring, ingenuity, and superiority at sea.

Perkins and Eleanor basked in the limelight but had more work to attend to. On October 20, they sailed out of San Francisco on the *Flying Cloud* on its first trip to China and then continued onward to New York, completing their circle of the globe on April 9, 1852. Perkins and Eleanor were now celebrities throughout the world. A grand celebration was held in their honor, and they returned to peaceful Marblehead for a rest before taking off in the fall for another sea journey to California and China.

Less than two years later, on January 21, 1854, Perkins and Eleanor sailed the *Flying Cloud* on its fourth trip from New York to San Francisco and arrived at the Golden Gate Bridge on April 20. At 89 days and 8 hours they had beat their own record by 16 hours. This record remained unbeaten by a sailboat until 135 years later when, in February 1989, *Thursday's Child*, a 60-foot racing yacht, made the passage in 80 days. *Flying Cloud's* record has yet to be bested by any commercial sailing vessel.

By 1855, Perkins and Eleanor decided they deserved a rest from the grueling life of sailing and retired to Massachusetts. Later, after the start of the Civil War, Perkins served the Union navy as captain on two different clipper ships before he and Eleanor returned to retirement on their farm near Salem.

In 1871 Perkins died at the age 57, but Eleanor lived for another 29 years. As for the *Flying Cloud*, it made many more voyages until it ran aground in 1874 in Saint John's, Newfoundland, Canada, and was salvaged for its metal fastenings. Like a good racehorse, the *Flying Cloud* raced best with a good navigator and captain. Eleanor Creesy's exceptional skill in plotting the fastest course made the *Flying Cloud* the most famous clipper ship of all time, and Eleanor's intelligence, courage, and grace set an example of what a woman could accomplish at sea.

Kay Cottee

ALONE ON THE HIGH SEAS

> *"I had firmly decided on an attempt to fulfill my dream—to be the first woman to sail single-handed, nonstop around the world."* —Kay Cottee

The sound of chattering and splashing dolphins awakened Kay Cottee several hundred miles off the coast of Brazil. They were surrounding her yacht: six at the stern, six on each side, and a few ahead of the bow. It had been only two days since Kay had crossed the equator, and in just two more days she would reach the halfway point of her round-the-world journey. Kay dashed below to grab her camera to take a photo of this strange escort, but when she returned on deck she was startled to see two of the largest whales she had ever seen headed straight for the boat. She desperately spun the wheel to change the boat's course, then with great relief watched as the whales dove just in time. They had been so close that their immense tails vanished into the sea only yards away from her. Within 20 minutes her dolphin escort disbanded, and it occurred to Kay

Kay Cottee's ship, the *First Lady*, at sea.
Courtesy of Kay Cottee

that maybe the dolphins had formed a shield around the *First Lady* to ward off the whales.

If anyone was destined to make her mark as a sailor, it was Kay Cottee, who was born in Australia on January 25, 1954. When Kay was only two weeks old, her parents, Jim and Joy McLaren, took her on her first sail in the company of her four big sisters. Kay's childhood home in Sans Souci is a community south of Sydney located on a strip of land with bays on either side. When Kay was born, there were few homes and a lot of bush. Kay explored this scrubland and sailed almost every weekend with her family. When Kay was six years old, her father started building a 37-foot-long, wood-hulled yacht in their backyard. She spent day after day watching him. With fascination she keenly observed each stage of boat construction. Three years later, when the yacht was finished, her parents christened it *Joy Too*. Each weekend from then on Kay, her four sisters, and her mother joined Jim McLaren and his crew as they raced the *Joy Too* in Sydney Harbor.

Two years later, the McLarens moved to a waterfront house on Kogarah Bay. By this time Kay was bored with school, and sailing was her singular passion. She looked forward to sailing every chance she could get. When her father gave Kay and her sisters a well-used 11-foot racing dinghy for Christmas, she was the only one who wanted to sail it. It handled easily, was ideal for learning how to race solo, and flew through the water in strong winds. Day after day Kay sailed her VJ-class dinghy until a young man named Phillip moved next door. His barebones racing craft, called a "skate," was even faster than her boat. It literally skimmed over the sea. Kay spent many days crewing with Phillip, who later married her older sister Elaine.

Each day at school Kay gazed out the classroom windows at the sea, daydreaming about sailing across the ocean. At home, instead of studying, she built model boats. Despite this lack of academic attention, she passed the exam for her intermediate certificate. Thus at the age of 16 she dropped out of school, having decided that she'd had enough education. A year later Kay entered secretarial school just as her sisters had done before her. It now appeared that the girl who dreamed of sailing had settled for a traditional life, especially after she married Neville Cottee, the son of one of her father's racing teammates. Neville was nine years older than Kay and worked in his family's plumbing business. She and Neville not only moved into a small apartment next door to his parents but also ate meals with them. Both worked in the family business. He worked as a plumber and Kay as a secretary in the family's cramped office. Neville's humorless parents disapproved of her vibrant, fun-loving personality which had been so appreciated at her home. Kay soon felt smothered by this new life. She began to question if it was the life she was destined to live and wondered if she could still become the adventurous sailor she had long dreamed of being.

The first step in changing her path came when she and Neville bought the hull of 22-foot sailboat, docked it in a marina, and moved aboard. Living conditions were cramped, but at least they were on their own. Away from his family they enjoyed the company of another young sailing couple who lived at the marina. Each day away from Neville's family during the three months it took to make the boat seaworthy allowed Kay's sense of purpose to slowly resurface. After the boat was ready, she and Neville set off on a cruise. Kay loved the journey, but it was all too brief. Before she knew it she was back to the same old job and stifling life with the in-laws.

After this taste of freedom, Kay was now motivated to take another step toward her goal by building a bigger boat. She and Neville soon began construction on the hull of a 36-foot yacht. After that was completed, Neville returned to plumbing, but for another 13 months Kay continued working on the yacht. She completed one task after another, from installing the deck and masts, to outfitting the cabin, to setting up the rigging. Local male boat builders were impressed by Kay's skill and knowledge. By the time the yacht, christened *Whimaway*, was launched, Kay was a minor celebrity among the Sydney boating community. This was exactly what she and Neville needed to get their new charter business on its feet. It also was what Kay required to make an escape from her unhappy life. Running the charter business allowed Kay to earn an income. She left Neville and slept on the yacht, in her car, or at a sister's home until she found an apartment. At the age of 27, Kay was on her own for the first time, and it felt just right.

She and Neville sold the yacht and split the money. In a stroke of luck, the *Whimaway*'s new owner asked Kay to continue managing the yacht as a charter boat, and soon other yacht owners made similar requests. Kay not only had a new career, but she also possessed a newfound confidence in managing her own life.

Now Kay was ready to focus on preparing to become the first woman to sail solo, nonstop, and unassisted around the globe. When a friend offered the use of his 35-foot yacht for two weeks in exchange for staying in her apartment, Kay readily accepted the offer. Her friend Linda agreed to help Kay sail on the 440-mile trip across the Tasman Sea to Lord Howe Island. Because Linda could only join Kay on the journey to Lord Howe Island, Kay had to sail back alone. During the entire 62-hour voyage she stayed awake and discovered, despite the lack of rest, that she loved sailing solo. Kay, now ready to accomplish her goal of sailing around the world, sold her charter boat business and bought the hull and deck of a 36-foot cavalier offshore racing yacht.

"I started fitting it out between odd jobs on boats to pay for rent, food, and timber. By nature a bower bird, I had kept just about everything that had broken down on the charter yachts, and I spent weeks getting everything to work again: bilge and water pumps, stove, winches, and so on," Kay later recounted.

Kay had almost completed the construction when she decided to compete in the single-handed event in the Solo Trans-Tasman Yacht Race. Kay's outgoing personality would now work to her advantage. She sold Marcus Blackmore, the owner of Australia's leading health care products company, on the idea of sponsoring her in exchange for naming her yacht after one of his products, a facial cleanser named Cinnamon Scrub. With only three months to get the boat finished before the race, Kay worked around the clock. With the help of her parents and friends, *Cinnamon Scrub* was seaworthy by the beginning of January. Next, Kay qualified for the race by sailing solo for 500 miles. During the 10-day-long

Trans-Tasman race, Kay labored furiously, changing the sails 52 times and waking up once every hour during the night to check her course. Though she didn't win the race, she proved herself to be an exceptional solo sailor.

Now more determined than ever to circumnavigate the globe, Kay persuaded Marcus Blackmore to sponsor her around-the-world journey. She convinced him to support her financially and assist in raising funds for the Life Education Program. This organization, which promoted healthy lifestyles for young people, was excited to have Kay's help. In turn Kay would be a great role model for kids, giving her voyage more than just a personal focus.

First she had to prepare her yacht, now renamed *Blackmore's First Lady*, for the long sail ahead. Every part of the boat had to be checked to see if it would withstand the wear and tear of months on the high seas. Kay reinforced the keel and added extra watertight bulkheads. Radar and radar-detecting devices, needed for detecting large ships, were installed. She purchased and packed a six-month supply of food and water. Other provisions included emergency medical supplies and fuel for the generator and auxiliary motor. Also squeezed aboard were tools and materials needed to make repairs, including extra sailcloth. By the time Kay was finally packed, there was barely room for her to fit in the yacht's small cabin. However, this didn't concern her, because she knew space would open up as her food and water disappeared.

Kay also had to set up a communications network with her land support crew and with Peter Sutton of Showboat Productions, who would handle her publicity and set up interviews. She spent hour after hour double-checking every detail, no matter how minor, to ensure a successful journey.

Kay set sail on November 29, 1987.

"I looked out over the bow and across the waters, trying to picture what lay ahead. It seemed to me I was looking into the mouth of a long, long tunnel," she recalls in a book about the voyage. Before the end of her first week at sea, she had to face her first big challenge. For several days there had been squalls with torrential rain and 40- to 45-mile-per-hour gusts. These rough and variable conditions forced her to frequently change sails. This work was so time consuming she barely had enough time to navigate, keep a look out for ships, eat, and sleep. Next, for several days at the end of December, the *First Lady* was buffeted by 55- to 60-knot winds and big waves. It was a bone-jarring ride, and Kay began to worry as her yacht started showing signs of wear. She fixed a leak and attempted to stop the loud vibrating noise made by the wobbling of the shaft that connects the rudder to the steering wheel. Unable to stop the wobble, she had to hope the steering mechanisms would hold together through the rest of the voyage.

As she neared Cape Horn, at the southern tip of South America, the *First Lady* was once more battered by strong squalls. One was so powerful that it knocked the yacht over flat on its side. As soon as Kay picked herself up, she went out onto the deck secured in safety harnesses. There she saw a big crack in the boom, the long pole attached to the bottom edge of the mainsail. Between squalls, Kay lashed another pole onto the boom, hoping it would hold it together until she could do a proper fix after the weather calmed down.

On January 19, 1988, after two weeks of rough sailing and frigid weather, Kay finally rounded Cape Horn, Chile. Many shipwrecks have occurred in this treacherous passage, especially when it is shrouded in fog. Kay was finally blessed with sunny weather. As she sailed by the shore she marveled at the view of snow-capped mountains and at the black-and-white albatrosses that circled her yacht.

Kay had now entered the Atlantic Ocean, and she set her course north. The official route for a round-the-world sail required that she cross the equator and pass around both São Paulo and São Pedro islands, part of a chain of rocky islands 500 miles off Brazil's coast. When past this point Kay celebrated with wine and a meal of freshly baked bread and canned crab. She had made it halfway through her journey with very little damage to the boat—and without suffering unbearable loneliness.

She now had an immense stretch of water to cross on her route across the Atlantic to the Cape of Good Hope at the southern tip of Africa. During the few next weeks, she sailed through one squall after another, which allowed Kay to replenish her freshwater supply—she collected rainwater that poured off the mainsail. When the weather turned calmer, she caught up on sleep and started writing the first chapter of her book *First*

Kay relaxing during a break from bad weather.
Courtesy of Kay Cottee

Lady. Due to her new location, radio conditions were better, so she was able to communicate with friends. This helped stave off loneliness and allowed her to savor her journey. One calm, windless night Kay witnessed the most beautiful starry sky of the entire trip. "The sky was ink black except for millions and millions of stars all of which were reflected in the mirror of the ocean . . . everywhere I looked around, above, below, behind, there were stars shining," Kay describes in *First Lady*.

At the start of April, as the *First Lady* neared Cape Horn at the southern tip of Africa, Kay found herself sailing in rough seas again. The boat was tossed by immense waves and pummeled by strong winds. The noise became so deafening that Kay couldn't sleep. Then the winds blew harder, and the *First Lady* was soon dwarfed by waves as tall as five-story buildings. As Kay rocked about inside the cabin considering her precarious situation, she felt the bow rise higher and higher, until she sensed that the *First Lady* was almost standing straight up on one end. When the boat finally leveled out, Kay realized in horror that it was totally out of the water, suspended for a moment in the air. Instantly she braced her hands on the ceiling and her feet on the floor to avoid injury as the *First Lady* landed with a thunderous crash. Though she had avoided injury, Kay wondered if the boat had been damaged.

Secured by two harness lines, she scrambled on deck and discovered with relief that everything was intact. Two days later Kay rounded the cape in rough weather, but the worst was not over yet. Less than a week later she was struggling to control the *First Lady* as the yacht raced along, propelled by 75-mile-per-hour winds. All of a sudden the *First Lady* was knocked over flat, the mast plunged underwater. Caught in the grip of a mammoth wave, the boat was pushed along in this position until it was able to right itself. Clothes and gear were scattered about the cabin. Water poured in from an open hatch. Kay secured the hatch and was busy bailing out the water when the boat was knocked flat again. Laying atop her scattered belongings, with her kettle and other items from the galley flying through the air, she couldn't help but laugh.

When righted, the *First Lady* continued to roar along at high speed. Kay realized she must decrease the speed to avoid damaging her vessel. In the inky darkness, she scrambled onto the deck, secured by harness lines, to check for any damage. In the strong winds the raindrops striking her hands felt as sharp as knives. Just as she was adjusting the sails and preparing to drop the anchor to slow down her yacht, she noticed a light in the distance. Realizing that she was on a collision course with a large ship, Kay turned on the lights and set off a flare to alert them of her presence. Trembling in fear, she watched as the massive vessel passed within 1,000 feet of her small craft. Moments later her boat was knocked over again, and Kay found herself washed overboard and plunged underwater. As she held her breath she felt as if her lungs might burst. Suddenly the boat righted itself, yanking her out of the water and washing her back onto the deck. Kay was now utterly exhausted and battered from head to toe, but she was alive and determined to sail on.

On June 5, 1988, Kay sailed past the finish line in Watsons Bay and into Sydney Harbor where she was greeted by tens of thousands of people, including her family, friends, the prime minister's wife, and the premier of New South Wales. This was a powerful experience after 189 days alone at sea. On shore Kay was awarded the Australian of the Year Award and appointed an Officer of the Order of Australia.

Peter Sutton, who had served as the publicist for her round-the-world sail, now took on the job of her manager as she started her new role as a public speaker, working to raise $1 million for the Life Education charity. In 1989 Kay published *First Lady*, the book about her journey; many years later she wrote another book about her life after her return home, *All at Sea on Land*. Peter and Kay married shortly after her trip, and together they have a son, Lee. Kay's courageous journey became an ongoing inspiration to other women who dream of sailing solo around the globe.

Edie Widder

INTO THE DEEP, DARK SEA

> *"Little dots like fairy dust, splats like puffs of liquid, sparks like embers thrown up by a campfire emerged from the dark. Except all these lights were blue. It was absolutely mesmerizing, and I couldn't believe how much there was. It was everywhere."* —Edie Widder

E dith "Edie" Widder was inside a Deep Rover submersible 500 feet below the surface of the Pacific Ocean when she heard a high-pitched sound. Something wasn't right. She leaned to the side, noticed water on the floor, and realized she had to act soon before her single-person sub became too heavy to operate. Fortunately, Edie was an experienced submersible pilot and knew if she blew out the ballast and jammed on the thrusters she would be able to slowly return to the surface. It then occurred to her that the shipboard controller for the dive must have removed a handle for a valve that lets in the seawater necessary to operate an emergency pump used to make drinking water. This water was needed only if the sub was trapped underwater. Edie replaced the handle but was unable to shut the valve. Luckily, despite the leak, she was able rise to the surface.

In June 1951, the Widder family celebrated the birth of little Edith, the family's long-awaited second child. By this time her brother, David Charles, was almost 11 years old. Her 53-year-old father, Dr. David Widder, and her 42-year-old mother, Dr. Vera Widder, were both mathematicians. He taught at Harvard University, and she had just taken leave of her post at Tufts College to be a full-time mother while Edith was young.

The Widder home in Arlington, Massachusetts, though close to Boston, bordered Spy Pond. This was where young Edie discovered turtles, water snakes, ducks, and the joy of tree climbing. After her 10th birthday she set the goal of climbing every tree around the shore. Because the pond was immense, it took most of the summer to accomplish this feat. Growing up in the Widder home was like being in a magical school where there were no tests or homework, only curiosity, questions, and exciting discussions. Edie was bright, but her parents and older brother were so intelligent that in comparison she felt dim. The school that Edie attended bored her so much that she had plenty of practice daydreaming. She didn't feel like exerting any effort, and her report cards reflected this.

When Edie was 11 years old, she traveled around the world for a year with her parents while her father was on sabbatical. They stayed for six months in Kew, Australia, a small town near Melbourne, where Edie finally discovered that school could be exciting. Numerous tree houses dotted the school grounds where Edie and other students went for snack breaks to eat oranges. On mini–field trips with her teacher and classmates near the school, they found a great variety of animals, including a few venomous snakes and spiders.

The Widder family stopped in Fiji on the way back to Boston, and it was there that Edie found her life's mission. The brightly colored fish and exotic sea creatures living in the coral reefs thrilled her unlike anything she had seen before. From that moment on she wanted to spend her life exploring the oceans. After she arrived home, Edie was committed to doing well in school so she could become a marine biologist. When she told her junior high guidance counselor of her desire to study biology, he assumed she wanted to become a nurse. He couldn't understand that she might want to take biology for any other reason. It wasn't until high school that she found her mentor in Harry Meserve, a truly remarkable biology teacher. Harry not only entertained his class with jokes and trained his students to become scientists, but he also encouraged them to ask their own questions. Unlike the counselor, Harry understood Edie's passion for becoming a biologist and gave her special attention. She attended his after-school hematology lab, where students learned techniques for analyzing blood samples. One day Harry asked Edie and another student, David Charles Smith, to help chaperone freshman students. She and this young man with the same name as her brother had many common interests. Edie soon realized that Harry had set them up on a blind date of sorts, and it worked. After graduation, Edie and David became husband and wife.

After high school, Edie studied biology at Tufts University while David served in the US Navy. Though becoming a marine biologist had been her goal, she didn't have any role models and did not believe that she could actually make a living exploring the oceans. After her graduation from Tufts, Edie found work at Harvard Medical School. Her boss was an eccentric and unpredictable French doctor working in electron probe microanalysis. This was a technology used to measure the chemical composition of infinitesimal quantities of solid substances. Edie excelled at this fussy, exacting work, but her life was not meant to be restricted to a lab.

Fate intervened two years later when David was discharged from the navy. He decided to study photography at a school in Santa Barbara, California, and Edie applied to an innovative program in electrical engineering at the University of California campus there. After they arrived she was surprised to find out she had been accepted with a scholarship to another program similar to the one she actually wanted to study. When she attempted to rectify this mistake, she was thwarted by the head of the innovative program. Though this was the mid-1970s, he wanted to bar female students studying in his program. Cleverly Edie found her way around this barrier by studying biochemistry and auditing classes in electrical engineering. At this point in her life she had no idea that this course of study would give her the knowledge and skills to explore a whole new frontier in marine biology.

The closest that Edie felt she could get to making a living studying marine life was through a degree in neurobiology, which would allow her to do laboratory studies on the nervous systems of marine animals. For her PhD thesis she monitored the electrical activity that sets off the production of light in a bioluminescent dinoflagellate. These minute organisms produce light through the same chemical reaction that fireflies use to light up summer nights. As she was about to finish her degree, Jim Case, her major professor, used grant money to purchase an expensive new gadget for measuring the color of very faint flashes of light produced by bioluminescent animals. Edie was always interested in new technology and couldn't keep her hands off it; she soon learned how to operate the device. Because Edie was the only one who knew how to use it, Jim invited her on one of his marine biology cruises to collect and measure the light of bioluminescent animals caught in trawling nets.

"Suddenly, I was doing what I had always dreamed of doing: going to sea on exploratory expeditions! The animals brought up in the nets were fantastic, and their light-producing capabilities were incredible. I was enthralled, but I still didn't see how I could carve a career out of this new passion," Edie later told an interviewer.

Her most exciting opportunity came next during a cruise organized with Dr. Bruce Robinson, who invited her to test a diving suit called the WASP. This specialized diving gear had been developed and used by the oil industry for work in offshore oil exploration. Unlike old diving suits, this one was roomy enough to have a display in front of the diver's face with dials, gauges, and switches. Now Edie had the chance to see for herself where bioluminescent organisms lived in the deep sea. On her first dive to 800 feet below the surface, she switched off the lights. The experience was unforgettable. "There were explosions of light everywhere, like being in the middle of a silent fireworks display," Edie described to an interviewer.

Edie dives in the WASP suit to study bioluminescent organisms.
Courtesy of Edie Widder

Later, on another dive in the Wasp, she had the suit's lights out when she brushed against a 30-foot-long chain of jellyfish. This triggered a bioluminescent reaction that was so bright she could read all the dials and gauges in her suit. Now Edie was totally hooked on exploring the light-making organisms of the deep ocean. She had dozens of questions and was anxious to find the answers.

Edie traveled on research expeditions along the coasts of California, Hawaii, Maine, northwest Africa, and Costa Rica. On many of these scientific explorations, trawling nets were used to catch deep-sea animals. This technique fails to reveal any clues about the habitats, behaviors, and relationships of these creatures. Scuba diving and submersibles allow biologists to actually enter deep-sea environments, but Edie knew that they still were not the best way to make new discoveries.

Edie works in the rear chamber of the Johnson-Sea-Link submersible.
Courtesy of Edie Widder

"All these things are noisy, with big lights. So how many things are there in the ocean that we don't know about, because we've scared them away?" Edie wondered.

On dives in the Deep Rover, Edie turned off the lights and tried her best to trim out the buoyancy so that the sub's movement didn't cause the animals to light up. Later she invented SPLAT (Spatial Plankton Analysis Technique), a one-meter wide hoop covered with a screen that attaches to the front of the sub. When animals bump into it, they emit light. After using it for a while, she was able to identify individual species by the type of flash they made. She soon understood that by collecting more data like this she would discover not only the existence of new animal species but also how abundant they were, where they lived, how they behaved, and most important, how they used bioluminescence for survival.

After earning her doctorate, Edie stayed at UC–Santa Barbara for the next seven years as a postdoctoral student working with Jim Case. Edie hoped to develop more sophisticated instruments, and her wish came true when the navy asked Case to devise a way of measuring marine bioluminescence. The partnership was a perfect one.

"The navy wanted to know how much light there was, and I wanted to know who's making it and figure out the ecology. I wanted to go to a chunk of ocean and say, 'Oh, it's all copepods here,' or whatever," Edie told a journalist in 2004.

If a boat, submarine, or Navy Sea, Air, and Land (SEAL) scuba diver triggered light-producing organisms in the sea it could alert an enemy of its presence. Any kind of motion, whether from a diver, landing craft, or submarine, can stimulate plankton to glow. In November 1918, the last German U-boat that was sunk during World War I was spotted because the bioluminescence it stirred up in the Mediterranean Sea gave away its location. If the navy could chart not only where these bioluminescent organisms were present but also their numbers and the periods when they were most abundant, they would be able to avoid detection during nighttime maneuvers.

First, with the help of engineers, Edie coinvented the Hidex, a meter that measures marine bioluminescence, and then LoLAR, an even more sensitive meter. However, it was her poetically named Eye of the Sea that led to the biggest discoveries. This remotely operated camera is able to rest on the ocean floor, where it records the species present, their numbers, and their behavior. On its very first trial run in the Gulf of Mexico, it hit pay dirt. Using light that imitated a jellyfish's call for help, Edie made a discovery.

"Exactly 86 seconds after we turned it on, we recorded a six-foot-long squid that's so new to science it can't even be placed in any known family. I couldn't have asked for a better proof of the concept," Edie reported. Over the years Edie and other marine biologists revealed that more than 90 percent of animals living in the deep sea were capable of producing light. She and her colleagues discovered an octopus with suckers that flash. They speculated these flashes attract small crustaceans, called copepods, like moths to a porch light, and thus provide the octopus with dinner. She found out that some fish, such as the cookie-cutter shark, use unique lures. This species has an unlit patch of skin outlined by sparkling light cells. These small lights give the unlit patch the shape of a small fish, which attracts much larger hunters such as tuna, swordfish, and porpoises. As these predators rush in to snatch the nonexistent fish, the shark bites off a chunk of their flesh. In addition Edie recorded evidence of fish using light for defense. For example, the shining tubeshoulder squirts light from its shoulder tube that is so bright it blinds attackers. Other organisms, such as minute dinoflagellates,

Edie 33 feet underwater in the front dive sphere of the Johnson-Sea-Link submersible.
Courtesy of Edie Widder

light up the water, revealing approaching predators to larger ones.

In 2005 Edie cofounded the Ocean Research and Conservation Association (ORCA), where she began working with others to create new technologies used to protect and restore aquatic ecosystems and the species that inhabit them. In 2007, Edie received a MacArthur Fellowship for her pioneering studies—not only an affirmation of her discoveries, but perhaps a surprise to teachers who remembered Edie as a daydreaming girl in their classes so many years before.

In June 2012, Edie joined Tsunemi Kubodera, a squid expert and researcher for Japan's National Museum of Science and Nature, to dive in a submersible into deep waters of the North Pacific Ocean, near the Ogasawara archipelago south of Tokyo. In cooperation with the Discovery Channel and the Japanese TV network NHK, they searched for a giant squid, hoping to make a video recording of one in its habitat. They sighted one at a depth of 2,066 feet and pursued it down to a depth of 2,952 feet. Before it disappeared, they lured it with a smaller squid and then tested a device Edie created which mimics a bioluminescent jellyfish display. The light from the display attracted the squid, which located the prey using its basketball-size eyes. At that moment Edie, Tsunemi, and their crew recorded the elusive creature for the first time.

"All of us were so amazed at what it looked like. It looked carved out of metal. And it would change from being silver to gold. It was just breathtaking," Edie Widder told a reporter from the *Los Angeles Times*.

Though giant squid have washed up on shore and been caught in nets, this was the first time people could watch this deep-sea animal in its home. This was one more achievement for Edie and her colleagues, but there will likely be many more incredible discoveries as Edie continues to explore the deep, dark sea.

Jill Fredston

ROWING ALONG COLD COASTS

"I just launched my boat, clambered in, and rowed to a new freedom." —Jill Fredston

During the summer of 1986 Jill Fredston and Doug Fesler were traveling up the coast of British Columbia, Canada. He was paddling a sea kayak, and she was rowing an oceangoing rowboat. They had been traveling for more than four weeks when they reached the northern tip of Vancouver Island and had to cross the treacherous waters of Queen Charlotte Sound to continue onward. The huge swells made their progress slow, but it was the enormous swirling whirlpools that were truly horrifying. These occur when larger swells touch the ocean bottom where reefs are located. Large enough to swallow their boats, these vortex-like holes had to be avoided. As their boats rode the rolling swells, Jill and Doug were seldom able to sight the holes until they were almost upon them. It was like traveling through a minefield. Jill felt more afraid than she had ever felt before but knew she had to stay focused as she steered her boat past one whirlpool after another. As the daylight faded,

Jill rowing during warm weather.
Courtesy of Doug Fesler

she and Doug realized they had to reach the shore soon and started to search for a safe passage through the heavy high surf to the beach. Doug, who was in the lead, suddenly sighted a narrow corridor between a small island and a reef. He patiently waited for a set of smaller waves to roll in and then raced through the gap. As Jill followed, she was slammed by a monster wave. Before the next wave could pound her, she desperately used all her might to turn her waterlogged craft and was able to reach the safety of the shore.

Jill Fredston was born on the very first day of 1958. In 1968, when she was just a skinny little 10-year-old living in a waterfront home in Larchmont, New York, she received her very own boat. This gift from her parents was a small type of rowboat called a pram. Jill was so overjoyed that she endured the teasing her parents gave her by naming it the *Ikky Kid*. In the *Ikky Kid* Jill explored every cove and inlet of Larchmont harbor. One day, when she was in junior high, she rowed up a waterway to her school. It was low tide when school let out and the *Ikky Kid* was beached high and dry. Over the years she would learn about reading tide charts as well as boating hazards.

"I do know, from the moment I stepped into *Ikky Kid*, I sensed the potential of using my own power to compose my life. *Ikky Kid* floated me to new horizons, away from the circle of competitive, achievement-oriented friends, giving me room to find good company in myself and in nature," Jill Fredston recounts in her book *Rowing to Latitude*.

Jill's parents supported their daughter's adventuresome nature. One summer they even sent her to a ranch camp in Wyoming where Jill transformed from a suburban New Yorker into a rough and ready cowgirl. She learned to handle a horse as if she had grown up riding one. She started saying "crik" instead of "creek" and brandished an unopened can of snuff in her back pocket, just like the locals did. The following summer, at a National Outdoor Leadership School class (NOLS), Jill learned how to camp in the mountains and set up a tent in the backyard after returning home to Larchmont. At 16, Jill worked with other Student Conservation Association volunteers repairing a trail in Yosemite National Park. The weeks she spent near a high pass, miles from the nearest road, cultivated her love of wild, open places and the desire to protect them. The following summer, on her next NOLS program, Jill paddled a sea kayak through Alaska's Prince William Sound. During the outing she and five other boaters came so close to a group of killer whales that they were showered in whale spout. They returned home smelling like rotten fish. For once she truly was an icky kid.

After graduation from high school, Jill enrolled at Dartmouth College in New Hampshire. During her first days there, she was bewitched by a new type of boat, a 60-foot-long rowing scull. In it were eight sliding seats, one for each of the rowers. At the stern was a fixed seat for the coxswain, the team member who steers and directs the team as the rowers propel the scull forward. On Dartmouth's crew team Jill learned to use her whole body—arms, legs, and back—on each and every stroke of the 13-foot-long oars. All the teammates did their best to row in synchrony. When all 16 oars moved together as one, the scull surged forward with the coordinated power. Little by little Jill and her fellow boat mates developed the coordination, strength, and stamina to row harder and longer than they had ever imagined possible.

"We became one long, gasping body with 16 muscled arms and knotted calves," Jill later recalled.

Going beyond what they thought possible and exerting every last bit of energy were necessary. Sometimes, races were won by mere inches. Jill loved the discipline of sculling but wasn't sure if it suited her. She sensed that she could be a better long-distance rower than a short-distance sprinter.

After graduating from Dartmouth, Jill's compass pointed her toward colder regions. She spent a winter in the Colorado Rockies and a summer on Greenland's ice fields learning about glaciers before beginning her graduate studies at the University of Cambridge's Scott Polar Research Institute in Cambridge, Great Britain. Once more Jill found herself crewing, but this time it was on a four-woman team. Crewing in Great Britain turned out to be a very different experience. Here women athletes didn't compete at the same level as those in the United States. Nor was it considered proper for female scientists to be members of polar research expeditions. Jill silently seethed when the former head of the Polar Institute stated that women should not participate in these expeditions because they were a distraction to the male scientists. After Jill was awarded her master's degree in 1982 she took off for Anchorage, Alaska. She was look-ing for work and ready to boat in wilder waters. Sea kayaking was becoming popular, but Jill was a rower. Because oceangoing rowboats were not then being made, she customized an 18-foot fiberglass rowboat. By adding a deck and watertight bulkheads (for stowing gear and supplies) Jill made it more seaworthy. This new rowboat handled differently than any others she had rowed. With practice she gradually developed new techniques and was soon rowing gracefully through Alaskan waters.

"A good rowing stroke is fluid, circular, and continuous. It is unmarred by pauses, lurches, yanks, or back heaves," Jill said about this skill.

Even though Jill knew very little about avalanches, she landed a job as a snow and ice specialist at the Arctic Environ-mental and Research Center, a department of the University of Alaska in Anchorage. When the university won the contract for the Alaska Avalanche Forecast Center, her boss appointed her as its director. Despite her lack of experience with avalanches, he was confident that she could "learn whatever she needs to." To accomplish this Jill spent hour after hour in the field examining avalanches with the assistance of Alaska's avalanche guru, Doug Fesler. Doug's deep knowledge came from years of investigat-ing avalanches in the field. At first he doubted that Jill, being so new to the hazardous field of avalanche study, had what it took to become an expert. Jill was doggedly determined to learn what she had to and prove him wrong. With Doug's help she discovered how to analyze each avalanche she investigated. She witnessed tragic destruction of property and human lives and helped search for survivors. Little by little she began to under-stand the conditions that create different types of avalanches. Over time she developed the skill to not only predict when avalanches might occur but also what type and size they might be. Slowly Doug became impressed with her ability. Gradually their relationship shifted from strictly professional to a friendship and then to something more serious.

As Jill settled into her new life in Anchorage, she built a cabin on the outskirts of town. Doug helped with the construction and then moved in with her. Now Jill was living in the kind of "wild place" she had yearned to live in as a young woman. She had a house, a partner to explore with, and a new rowboat with a durable Kevlar shell that she christened *Princess*. Best of all, with a length of 20 feet and three watertight bulkheads, it could hold three months of food, supplies, and gear. Doug was an experienced kayaker, and so they decided to set off on a long sea voyage from Seattle, Washington, up the coast of British Colombia and through the Inside Passage to Skagway, Alaska. The scenery was majestic. There were hazards, hardships, and blissful days in serene settings. The trip turned out to be a success for them, both as boaters and as a couple. Thus began the first of many summers spent exploring northern coasts.

The next summer Jill and Doug followed the Yukon River from its headwaters at Tagish Lake to the Bering Sea, a distance of 2,000 miles. Their departure was on the longest day of the year, when the sun barely sets in the far north. Sixty-nine days later, the journey ended at Nome, Alaska, across Norton Sound from the mouth of the Yukon, as darkness arrived early in the evening. It was a long, peaceful, and poetic trip during which they met warmhearted people in remote villages along the shore.

"The river speaks a language rich in verbs—it is constantly rippling, sliding, bubbling, and bending. Perhaps for that reason it made me feel very much alive," Jill wrote of this experience.

Jill and Doug hoped to continue along the coast from Nome the next summer and paddle to the northernmost point of Alaska, Point Barrow, but the winter of 1987–88 delivered more than the normal number of avalanches. This caused them to be so busy with their work as avalanche experts that they were unable to depart on the planned date. In the end they had only 45 days to complete the trip, so they chose to launch instead from Kotzebue, on the Seward Peninsula, many miles north of Nome.

They were in the far north, where weather conditions could become deadly at any time of the year. After leaving Point Hope they traveled along the coast of the Chukchi Sea. Without much warning the weather shifted, and they were paddling through a raging sea with 15-foot waves pounding the shore. On land, torrential rains flooded the tundra, and 45-mile-per-hour winds, with even fiercer gusts, twisted their tent almost to the breaking point. While they were waiting out the worst of the storm in their tent, a brown bear pressed a paw onto the nylon tent fly mere inches above Jill's head. Fortunately, after Jill and Doug both shouted, "Hey, bear!" the huge creature left them alone. There were other memorable events yet to come. While launching his kayak from shore, Doug was pummeled by surf. As they paddled below a sea cliff where kittiwakes were nesting, irate gull-like birds bombarded them with streams of bird droppings. Then, early one morning, they were awakened when a bear demolished their tent with two powerful whacks. Like the previous bear, they were lucky it left them unharmed.

As they traveled along the coastline, they observed wolves, foxes, and bears going about their daily routines. The scenery varied from endless stretches of tundra to calm lagoons, to sea cliffs that towered hundreds of feet above the shore. Doug and Jill pulled into tiny villages where they made friends with locals. Without regular baths Jill truly was once again an icky kid, but Doug didn't mind—he smelled just as bad.

As the days passed by at this far northern latitude, winter approached rapidly. Their trip soon became a race against time.

Just as they neared Point Barrow, strong headwinds slowed their progress and quickly formed pack ice that blocked their route. There was no other option but to retreat to their last stopover at Point Lay. Had they continued they might have become trapped in thick pack ice like the three gray whales that were stranded near Point Barrow a week or so afterward.

Traveling together for months at a time was not always easy, but in the end it created an inseparable bond. Doug and Jill felt like they were made for each other and celebrated in 1989 with a wedding at Jill's parents' house in Larchmont.

In 1991, Jill and Doug followed the Mackenzie River west from Great Slave Lake in Canada's Northwest Territories, where mosquitoes were so abundant that they had to wear head nets and gloves at all times. After completing the 1,100-mile journey to Beaufort Sea, they steered west to reach Point Barrow, Alaska. For nine days they proceeded through fog so thick they could barely see the shore. Again they encountered floes of pack

Jill navigating through and over the pack ice.
Courtesy of Doug Fesler

ice. Day by day the space between the floes narrowed until there was barely any open water. While trying to leap across a gap in the ice, Jill fell into the frigid water. By quickly stripping down and pulling on extra clothes she had kept dry for such an occasion, she avoided dying of hypothermia.

Eventually they encountered a continuous sheet of unbroken ice that stretched in front of them as far as they could see. Unlike the smooth surface of an ice rink, this frozen seawater was rough and strewn with enormous blocks of ice, some as tall as two-story houses. Not willing to turn back, they began the exhausting task of dragging their heavy boats over the ice. This became their routine for the next two weeks. On some days they were only able to haul the boats a mile or so. Finally as they approached Prudhoe Bay, the sea opened up again, the winds died down, and the temperatures rose to an almost tropical-feeling 50°F. When they reached the tiny town of Barrow they felt as if they had arrived at a metropolis. Here there was a Laundromat, showers, and a plane to fly them home.

During the next few years Jill and Doug continued to follow the northern coasts of the Northwest Territories, Labrador, Scandinavia, and Greenland. Each of these journeys left them with unforgettable memories. In 16 summers of boating they had traveled about 25,000 miles in their boats, all under their own power. This was more than the circumference of the Earth. In 2011 they put their avalanche work on hold and motored out of Cordova, Alaska, on a 47-foot cruiser with two rowboats on deck, headed south to the coasts of South America. With Jill now in her 50s and Doug in his 60s, they have gone on regular excursions along the coasts of Patagonia, Argentina, and north to Brazil using the large cruiser as a comfortable home base. They now have more time for adventures and many more miles of coastlines to explore.

Stephanie Schwabe

DIVING INTO THE DARK FRONTIER

> *"You feel like the clutter of the surface is gone. It's quiet, almost like arriving on another planet. You forget who you are because there is nothing like you in there." —Stephanie Schwabe*

Stephanie Schwabe's measurement indicated that the black hole she was about to explore was more than 150 feet deep. Unlike the black holes found in space, this black hole was a vertical cave system filled with water. As she descended into the dark water, Steffi halted at a depth of 60 feet after contacting what she thought was a mud floor. She was shocked when she reached down to find that instead of a floor there was only heat. When she plunged a leg down into the floor-like surface it jiggled like Jell-O. Then, as she submersed her whole body, she was suddenly enveloped in total darkness. What was this strange world she had ventured into?

Stephanie Schwabe was born January 1, 1957, in Flensburg, a German city on the border with Denmark. Her father, Christian Schwabe, was a dentist. Her mother had a son, Michael,

A rare sighting of Stephanie Schwabe out of the water.
Courtesy of Stephanie Schwabe

from her previous marriage. He was seven years older than Steffi. When she was a toddler the family moved to Iowa. Life at home was not easy. Her father was often brusque, and her severely depressed mother was distant. Like other troubled children, Steffi retreated into a shell. She found comfort in nature and imagined being small enough to walk between blades of grass and explore it like a forest.

Not long after moving to the United States, Steffi's father left dentistry to earn a doctorate in microbiology. When it came time for her to enter school, she was not allowed to enroll because of her limited English. Her mother protested, but it was not until a year later that Steffi was finally permitted to start her schooling.

The family then moved to Boston when Dr. Schwabe became a professor at Harvard University. Steffi was both a year older and much taller than her fellow classmates. As a result of English being her second language, her shy nature, and her struggles with dyslexia, school was difficult. She soon became the target of school bullies. Though she learned how to fight off physical attacks, the teasing hurt. At home her father berated her, calling her stupid so often she soon believed him. Her situation got even worse when her brother, Michael, began to harass her, and there was no one to whom she could report his behavior. But in sports, she was sure of her abilities. She loved to swim but was plagued by reoccurring ear infections.

About the only time Steffi spent with her father was when they went sailing. She was never at ease in his company, but she loved to sail. As the boat cruised along the water's surface, she imagined what it might be like in the dark depths below.

At the start of her teen years, the family moved to Charleston, South Carolina. School was still a challenge, but Steffi continued to excel in sports, especially swimming and sailing. She took classes at the College of Charleston through a special program at her high school and at age 16 became the youngest freshman ever to enter the college. At her parents' insistence she took classes to prepare for medical school. Steffi found these classes difficult, had no interest in becoming a doctor, and was only doing what her parents wished her to do. Finally deciding to make her own choices, she told them that she wanted to change her major. In turn they refused to continue paying for her tuition. Steffi dropped out of college and moved into a place of her own. She was happy to be away from her father and brother. She found work as a veterinary surgery specialist and considered becoming a vet.

One day at work, while Steffi was executing a complex procedure, she suddenly realized that every day she was competently completing the same tasks as fellow workers who had advanced college degrees. It was then that Steffi finally understood that she wasn't dumb.

At the age of 29, Steffi returned to the College of Charleston, where a chance encounter changed the course of her life. One morning, after her two-hour swim team practice, Steffi noticed a scuba class gathered by the pool. Despite her shy nature, she boldly walked up to the instructor and asked, "Could a person

with the lifelong ear troubles I have ever dive?" She was thrilled
by both his reply of yes and invitation to join the class.

Andy Hansen, the owner of Charleston Diver, was a kind and
talented scuba instructor. From the moment Steffi became his
student he gently taught her how to dive. Before long, she was
his star student and within a year had not only earned her master diver certificate but Andy's friendship as well. Steffi joined
Andy and his other students on dives into rivers west of Charleston and began working as his assistant by helping instruct the
newest divers. At the shop she maintained and repaired the
scuba gear. On her first ocean dive Steffi was mesmerized. As
she observed schools of colorful fish and investigated a ship-
wreck, it seemed as if time had stopped. Only the dial on her
air gauge indicated otherwise. Later she wrote, "In that short
period of time, I had become a dive junkie."

The next big shift in Steffi's life happened in June 1990, after
she received her geology degree. Her professor Jim Carew rec-
ommended that she become a graduate student of one of his former students, John Mylroie. John was a professor of geology at
the University of Mississippi and studied caves in the Bahamas.
Steffi was intrigued. She flew to the Bahamian island of San Salvador to meet John and tour his study site. From the start there
were challenges: It was her first flight on a small plane, and its
landing on the tiny airstrip was too much of a thrill. Soon after
arrival she received a painful bite from one of the San Salvador's
notorious horseflies. When she discarded her shoes to walk on
the sand, she stepped on spiny burs that pierced her soles. But
none of this dampened Steffi's enthusiasm. Not even the wild
man, wearing a loud shirt and straw hat, who sat down next to
her at lunch in the research center's cafeteria made Steffi recon-
sider why she was there. Without any introduction or greeting,
this fellow bluntly informed her that if she had any wish to fit

in that she must swallow, in one mouthful, an entire bowl of Jell-O. To demonstrate, he slurped up a bowlful and gulped it down. This madman turned out to be Dr. John Mylroie. Not put off by this odd display, Steffi joined him and other students on the afternoon field trip to Lighthouse Cave. The series of small underground chambers featured bat-covered ceilings and cockroach-coated walls. As she and the other students slogged through water fouled with bat and cockroach droppings, they had to take extra care to keep their mouths closed. Steffi took this all in stride and afterward signed on to be one of John's master's students.

At the University of Mississippi, Steffi immediately immersed herself in her coursework. One day in John's office she noticed two books about blue holes by a cave diver named Rob Palmer. She borrowed these and became intrigued by the description of the underwater cave systems. Unlike black holes, which are vertical and filled with inky black water, blue holes are horizontal, appear dark blue in contrast to the shallow water around them, and can be several miles in length. He claimed they were one of the planet's last unexplored frontiers. Steffi wanted to visit a blue hole and meet Rob Palmer to learn what she could from him. Her chance came two years later as Steffi was finishing up her master's thesis. She was attending a geology conference at the field station on San Salvador Island where she made a presentation about her studies of the cave rock in the Bahamas. She knew Rob Palmer would be arriving and hoped to meet him at the farewell party on the last evening of the conference. On the day of the party she lost track of time while out searching for new caves. Crawling about underground hour after hour had left Steffi with stained clothes and hair caked with mud and powdered with dust. By the time she returned to the station she was late. Instead of cleaning up, Steffi decided to head straight to the party. Oblivious of her appearance, she entered looking like some kind of cave creature. After the crowd erupted in laughter, Steffi made a quick exit. She showered, changed into more appropriate clothes, and this time entered looking like a pretty, young scientist. And there, deep in conversation with John, was Rob Palmer. She joined them, and before she knew it, she was taking Rob and some others to visit one of the smaller caves she had just discovered. During the walk there she and Rob chatted as naturally as if they were old friends. After the cave visit, a stop at the local tavern for beer, and snorkeling in the full moonlight, she and Rob ended up alone on a beautiful white sand beach. It was here on this magical night that Rob and Steffi fell instantly in love. From that moment on they were a couple. He was both Steffi's first close friend and first true love. The next day while gazing at Rob, a strange notion entered her mind; she thought, "This man would never grow old."

With her master's degree completed, Steffi shoved off for Great Britain to live with Rob in a "quaint" cottage. It was charming on the outside—and in winter it was an icebox on the inside.

Rob was well-known and respected for his cave explorations. He knew many geologists, including a professor who was interested in blue holes and taught at the prestigious University of Bristol. There happened to be a scholarship available at this university for a graduate student who would take courses in both geography and geology. Steffi applied and was awarded the scholarship.

Steffi was not comfortable during Great Britain's long winters. When Rob proposed marriage, Steffi accepted on the condition that he move with her to the Bahamas as soon as they could. At the small wedding Steffi dressed in a jacket with long tails, jeans, and cowboy boots, while all the men, including Rob, wore kilts.

Steffi was now busy taking classes in addition to beginning her investigation into the formation of underwater caves. On trips to the Bahamas she collected rock samples from caves, and back at Bristol she analyzed them in the university's well-equipped labs. Little by little, her data accumulated. Meanwhile, Steffi read about a discovery that Scottish stonemasons had made in the early 20th century: some bacteria could eat away the surface of rocks. This information would be important for Steffi in making her own discovery.

By the time Rob and Steffi moved to the Bahamas, she was immersed in writing her PhD thesis. She theorized that acids produced by a variety of bacteria species living in crevices in carbonate rock slowly dissolved the rock. Rainwater percolating from the surface into the rock transported these acids, which slowly created caves. In essence, Steffi showed that blue holes were the result of a biological process.

While Steffi wrote her thesis, Rob continued to explore blue holes and other underwater caves. To support these investigations and to ensure protection of these unique cave systems, they established the Blue Holes Foundation. She and Rob also worked together on film projects, such as one with a German film crew that documented Rob's discovery of a Lucayan ceremonial canoe. In it were artifacts and the remains of a person laid to rest. Because the Lucayan people had been enslaved and exiled by the Spanish five centuries before, Steffi and Rob knew that this find was extremely old.

In May 1997 Steffi bid Rob farewell at the airport as he left to spend two weeks in Egypt diving with friends in the Red Sea. Strangely, she wondered if she would ever see him again. Rob had always taught safe diving. He cautioned against ignoring the physical limits of deep water. At depths of 100 feet or more, divers can experience a condition called narcosis that causes confusion and a loss of coordination. At greater depths loss of consciousness and eventually death may occur. Despite his history of being a cautious diver, during this trip he spent much of his time making deep dives. One of his diving friends was concerned and wondered if Rob was trying to prove himself to the younger, more reckless divers who were breaking depth records. On his last dive, the friends he was diving with watched him continue down until he disappeared from sight. They never saw him again, and his body was never found. When Steffi heard the news, she fell to pieces. She later wrote, "It was like my spirit had stepped outside my body." Her husband, her lover, and her friend was gone. Healing from this loss would be a slow process, despite support from her friends and mother.

During the following few months, Steffi worked with film crews documenting caves such as Mermaid's Lair and Four Shark. During the filming of Four Shark, one of Rob's oldest diving friends, Rob Parker, an extreme diver and adventure cameraman, perished while exploring. Steffi had wanted to accompany Parker, fearing that he was not in the right condition to make the dive. Now, only three months after her husband's death, she suffered another loss.

Fortunately, a new adventure came her way to keep her looking forward. Pete Smith, the head of a new film production company, wanted to film Steffi on a new exploration. She suggested the black hole of Andros Island, a remote, unexplored cave. Years before, Rob Palmer had sighted a large, black, almost perfectly round hole as he flew over the island. He guessed that the black color was due to its great depth. On June 20, 1998, Steffi and Pete flew there in a seaplane. Pete filmed Steffi as she descended into the hole and was shocked when she disappeared into darkness. When she reappeared he noticed blackness flowing off her head like paint. Since they needed to fly back before

Steffi conducting tests before she
dives into the black hole.
Courtesy of Stephanie Schwabe

dark, the exploration was cut
short. Steffi was disappointed
at only being able to partially
explore the mysterious cave.

She wanted to return as
soon as she could. Her next
opportunity arrived about
one year later, when she was
working with an Australian
TV series called *Quest*. Two
of Rob's diver friends, Ron
and Andrew, were part of the crew. They were as anxious as she
was to explore the black hole. This time Steffi flew out to Andros
Island via a helicopter and brought a hydrolab to analyze the
water. When she lowered it down to the dark layer, the instrument indicated that the amount of dissolved oxygen was nearly
zero. She hypothesized that something in the layer was using
up the oxygen, perhaps an unknown organism. The instrument
also indicated the presence of the poisonous substance hydrogen sulfide. This time as Steffi descended, she was followed by
Andrew, and by Ron, who was filming. When she reached the
dark layer, her feet felt warm and she smelled the rotten egg
stench of the hydrogen sulfide. Despite Andrew signaling for
her to stop, she continued. After passing through the blackness,
she reached cool, clear water. From below, the dark layer had a
purple-orange color and resembled a science-fiction landscape.
The samples she brought back from this expedition contained a

new species of bacteria, which she named *Allocromatium palmerii* after Rob. Steffi theorized that this species of bacteria created the high water temperature in the dark layer.

During the next few years Steffi garnered new honors. She was made a fellow of the Royal Geographic Society, a member of the prestigious Explorers Club, and named as a NASA fellow in exobiology. She also received a Courage Award from the Wings WorldQuest organization.

As Steffi continued to investigate caves, she made more discoveries, such as revealing that bacteria in underwater limestone caves survive on nutrients in dust blown from the Sahara Desert, all the way across the Atlantic Ocean. In the sediments of these caves she detected toxic substances, such as PCBs and heavy metals, from industrial waste from Europe and North America that is incinerated in Africa and carried by winds to the Bahamas. Steffi's love of diving, curiosity, and scientific skills have confirmed that we live on a small planet full of big mysteries. Each new discovery only increases Steffi's desire to stick around as long as she can to ask more questions and dive in pursuit of answers.

"I saw recently that some other group says I'm considered a legend. I thought you had to be dead for that. Maybe they know something I don't," Steffi mused in an interview.

Steffi ready to dive
Guardian Fracture Cave.
Courtesy of Stephanie Schwabe

PART IV

LONG TREKS

Isabella Bird Bishop

HEALTH, HORSES, ADVENTURE

> *"My pack, with my well-worn umbrella upon it, was behind my saddle. I wore my Hawaiian riding dress, with a handkerchief tied over my face and the sun cover for my umbrella folded over and tied over my hat, for the sun was very fierce. The queerest figure of all was the would-be guide, with his one eye, his gaunt, lean form, and his torn clothes, he looked more like a strolling tinker than the honest worthy settler he is."* —Isabella Bird Bishop

In the spring of 1878 in Edinburgh, Scotland, Isabella Bird, a 47-year-old "spinster," was once again suffering from poor health. She had just received a marriage proposal from a proper gentleman, and she responded to it by departing on one more adventure to another part of the world.

This time Isabella was headed to Japan for an exploration off the beaten path, to places visited by few Europeans. During the three-month journey she traveled nearly 1,500 miles, most of it on horseback. She visited cities, ancient temples, and hot springs, but the most exciting part of the trip was staying in

Isabella in her Hawaiian riding dress.
Frontpiece A Lady's Life in the Rocky Mountains *1879 John Murray, London*

the home of an Ainu chief. The Ainu lived in Hokkaido, the northernmost island of Japan, where they had hunted and harvested food from the fields and forests for many centuries.

At the time of Isabella's visit, the Ainu were under the rule of the Japanese, who came from islands to the south. The Ainu were abandoning many of their traditions as they were forced to adopt Japanese customs. Isabella found Ainu culture fascinating. In her letters she described their intricate body tattoos, bark-fiber clothing, and bear-worshipping ceremonies. Despite referring to them as savages, Isabella felt comfortable and welcome in their community. As always, during this journey Isabella recovered her health and vitality.

Isabella Bird was born on October 15, 1831, into a prosperous middle-class family in Boroughbridge, England, within the heart of northern Great Britain. Her parents were members of the Clapham Sect, a group devoted to abolishing slavery. Her father, who was trained as a lawyer, served as a vicar in the parish church. Her mother, who grew up as the daughter of a vicar, taught at the Sunday school in her husband's church.

Isabella was sickly as a young girl. As was common during these times, her doctor prescribed outdoor activity as a cure, and in Isabella's case it proved successful. She adored horseback riding around the parish with her father, and by age 10 she could handle a full-size horse. She and her father had an especially close relationship. Isabella suffered from one illness after another. At the age of 23, her father gave her money to travel to the United States to visit relatives, hoping this would cure her most recent ailment. This journey was the start of her life of travel and travel writing. The letters she wrote to her family describing her travels were the foundation for her first book, *An Englishwoman in America*, published in 1856. Following her father's death two years later, she moved with her sister and mother to Edinburgh, Scotland. These years were uneventful as Isabella lived a quiet, homebound life. All this changed in 1868, when Isabella's mother passed away. All of a sudden she was free to live her own life. Her sister, Henrietta, moved to the Isle of Mull off the far-northwest coast of Scotland, but Isabella had other plans. Once again her health was poor. When her doctor suggested that she travel, Isabella was more than ready.

In July 1872, at the age of 40, Isabella sailed off for Australia and New Zealand, where she explored until the end of the year. On New Year's Day 1873, she boarded a barely seaworthy ship bound for Hawaii. During the passage they encountered a hurricane, and most of the passengers were terrified and seasick—but not Isabella. Under hardship and duress she rose to the occasion. She was the only one aboard willing and capable to care for a gravely ill passenger. For Isabella each day at sea was an adventure.

Before leaving Great Britain Isabella's back pain had been so severe that she had ceased horseback riding. In Hawaii she took to the saddle again, but now she sat astride the horse. In Great Britain only men rode this way, but on the islands most women had given up riding sidesaddle and replaced long riding dresses with more comfortable riding apparel. Life was freer in the

South Pacific, and Isabella quickly adapted to wearing bloomers and boots with spurs as she sat snugly on a Mexican saddle. As she explored Hawaii, her health improved day by day. This life, with fewer social restraints and more physical exercise, suited her. She was hosted by Hawaiians in their simple homes and climbed volcanoes to view eruptions. On the Big Island Isabella accepted an invitation from a man she had just met to join him in ascending Mauna Loa, the largest volcano on Earth. In a letter to her sister, she described her experience of sleeping in a tent at an elevation of more than 13,000 feet atop "the mightiest volcano in the world."

By then Isabella felt ready to visit the wild American West and boarded a ship bound for San Francisco. In her luggage was her special riding outfit composed of a half-fitting jacket, an ankle-length skirt, and Turkish bloomers. Tiring soon of the hustle, bustle, and frigid, foggy weather of San Francisco, Isabella traveled by train to the Rocky Mountains. In 1873 the region that now encompasses Rocky Mountain National Park was not easy to reach. The transcontinental railroad had just been completed, and Denver, Colorado, was still a small city. Isabella arrived in Cheyenne, Wyoming, and traveled south via stagecoach to Fort Collins, Colorado, where she managed to hire a guide who agreed to take her to the remote and reportedly beautiful Estes Park. Boastfully he informed her that he could find it blindfolded, but all he did was get them lost. By the end of the trip he had to rely on Isabella to lead them back to the nearest settlement, the frontier town of Longmont. There on the plains the heat was so unbearable that Isabella considered abandoning her goal of visiting Estes Park. However, she learned just in time of two young men who were about to ride there and arranged to accompany them. It took many miles of hard riding on a faint trail to arrive at a long gulch with broad meadows enclosed by pines, fir, and spruce. At the mouth of this narrow valley, dubbed Muggins Gulch, they found a crude log cabin. Out front of it stood a lovely mare and a large, growling collie. On the cabin's mud roof were the pelts of lynx, beaver, and other animals, which had been set out to dry.

Alerted by the barking dog, a grizzled-looking man, appearing more beast than human, emerged from the front door. His face would have seemed handsome except for his one empty eye socket. Isabella later wrote that he had "desperado" written all over him, but she forgot his appearance when he addressed them with the cultured voice of a gentleman. He served Isabella a cup of fresh water and related the story of how he lost his eye in a recent encounter with a grizzly bear. Later she found out that this new acquaintance had a reputation throughout the Colorado Territory as a daring scout and dangerous outlaw. She and Jim Nugent, also known as "Rocky Mountain Jim," would become close friends during Isabella's stay in the mountains.

Arriving finally in Estes Park, she and her companions came to the homestead of a Welshman by the name of Griffith Evans. He and his partner rented Isabella a log cabin where she had a view of the towering Longs Peak. It was unlike anything she had seen before, and she wanted to climb it as she had Mauna Loa. Taking advantage of the last of the mild weather, Rocky Mountain Jim offered to guide her there. They set off, with the two young men tagging along, carrying several days' worth of provisions in their saddlebags. By the following day they had gone as far as they could on horseback and continued on foot. After "leaping from rock to rock," they were halted by an impassable cliff. There was no choice but to backtrack and locate a better route. Each step they scrambled upward became more and more challenging for Isabella. Mountain Jim patiently encouraged her while they sought out footholds, sometimes on

Longs Peak.
Courtesy of Wikimedia Commons

minute knobs, and crawled on hands and knees along narrow ledges of cliffs that dropped off 3,000 feet to the slopes below. Isabella could proceed only by looking up, not down. Gasping for her breath, she finally reached the icy summit. Only two years before, Addie Alexander had become the first woman to summit the peak, and in mid-September 1873 Anna Dickinson had climbed the peak with the Hayden Expedition. Then Isabella became the third female to experience the spectacular view from the 14,259-foot peak.

During the next couple of weeks, Isabella spent hours in conversation with Mountain Jim. Though charmed by his gentlemanly manner and mountain-man roughness, she was frightened by his behavior whenever he drank whiskey.

As autumn passed, heavy snow carpeted Estes Park, and more was on its way. On October 20, Isabella packed her belongings and rode toward the plains on Birdie, her bay Indian pony.

Jim met her on the trail and wished her good-bye. It was a long ride to Denver, where Mrs. Evans graciously welcomed Isabella into her winter residence on the edge of the plains. Isabella soon tired of "civilization" and rode south to Colorado Springs. As she traveled solo she found shelter each night wherever she could, whether it be a rich man's ranch, a lonely settler's cabin, or a boardinghouse. On the first of November she turned north-ward toward the Great Divide of the Rocky Mountains. Back at Longmont she decided to return to Estes Park, where she would wait for Griffith Evans to arrive with some money he owed her. It turned out to be a long wait. Griffith and his partner had gone to Denver, leaving their ranch in the care of two young hunt-ers. Isabella spent her time riding through the mountains with Mountain Jim. On one of these outings he confessed his love for her, which had started on their climb of Longs Peak. Despite her warm feelings for him, Isabella refused his proposal to marry. Upset by her rejection, Jim claimed he would camp out in the hills until she departed and then galloped away. Though she was attracted to him, Isabella felt pity for the "ruin he had made of his life" and wrote, "He is a man any woman might love but no sane woman would marry."

After Griffith returned and Isabella's loan was repaid, Jim offered to escort her to the stagecoach stop 30 miles away on the plains and then bring Birdie back to the ranch. During her trav-els in Colorado she had ridden more than 800 miles, most of it over rough terrain. She had experienced extreme cold, hunger, and fatigue, but saying good-bye to Mountain Jim was the most difficult of all. Before he departed Isabella begged him to aban-don his wicked ways. Unable or unwilling to take her advice, he died a mere five months later in a gunfight.

Soon after Isabella returned to Edinburgh, John Bishop, a young doctor in his 30s, asked for her hand in marriage. As usual, once she was back at home, her health had declined. She didn't wish to be a sickly wife, so she packed her bags again and departed for a seven-month trek in Japan and five-month exploration of the Malay Peninsula. In 1880 her sister died, leaving her the only one in her family still living. Her sister's death was a great loss, and perhaps this was the reason she married John Bishop the following year. Despite her constant poor health, they lived a happy life together. He adored her, and when he was asked how such a frail woman survived her wild adventures, he said that she had "the appetite of a tiger and the digestion of an ostrich."

Tragically, Isabella found herself a widow just a few years later in 1886, when John suddenly passed away. As a cure for both her physical and emotional health, Isabella returned to her life of adventures. The first journey was through India, and next she rode her "hard, hungry, silver-grey Arab" horse through the high mountains and plateaus of Tibet for two months. This was followed by a trek in Persia, where she accompanied a British army survey. During this journey she traveled on a big mule along a mountain trail in a blizzard so fierce that she couldn't even see her mule's neck. Later, when she rode with hired muleteers into Kurdistan, "shrieking, yelling, and juggling" Kurdish horsemen rode alongside. A year after returning home from that journey to write a book and lecture about her travels, she became the first woman inducted into the Royal Geographic Society.

Isabella was unstoppable. Her next voyage was through China and Korea, where her mount was a Korean pony with an "evil glare in his eyes and a hyena-like yell" that rushed at any other ponies they came near. At age 70 Isabella visited Morocco and trotted for 30 miles per day on a stallion so large she needed a ladder to mount him. Only two years later, in 1903, with her bags packed for a return trip to China, Isabella fell ill. This time her condition was too severe to be cured by travel. When she died a year later, Isabella Bird left behind hospitals that she had helped establish in India, China, and Korea. Friends and admirers around the world mourned her passing. Her many sketches and photographs from her trips abroad, as well as the 14 travel books that she wrote, remain a testimony to her courage, curiosity, and boundless energy.

Annie Kopchovsky "Londonderry"

PEDALING AROUND THE WORLD WITH CHUTZPAH

> *"I stand and rejoice every time I see a woman ride by on a wheel. It gives her a feeling of freedom, self-reliance, and independence."* —Susan B. Anthony

On June 25, 1894, Annie Kopchovsky pedaled away from the Massachusetts statehouse in Boston on a new woman's bicycle donated by Columbia Manufacturing. Attached to the back fender was a placard advertising her sponsor, the Lithia Spring Water Company, promoting Londonderry Lithia Water. Calling herself Annie Londonderry, she promised to circle the world on her bicycle in 15 months. She wore a long, heavy skirt, which was not the most practical outfit for cycling but was what proper women wore at the time. With a weight of 42 pounds, her bicycle was more than a third of Annie's body weight, but it hadn't cost her a dime. It came equipped with hand brakes,

A studio portrait of
Annie before her trip.
Courtesy of Peter Zheutlin

but unlike modern bikes, it
didn't have a free-wheel system. Whenever she coasted,
the bike pedals continued to
spin around, making it necessary for her to place her feet on
the coaster brackets. At the same time she had to be careful to
keep her skirt from becoming entangled in the wheels.

During the latter half of the 1800s women were accomplishing remarkable feats. They scaled high peaks, journeyed
to remote rain forests, and trekked across distant deserts.
The majority of them were not only well educated, but they
were also financially well off. Annie was neither. She lived in a
cramped apartment in one of the poorest neighborhoods of Boston. She; her husband, Max; and their three children lived there
with her older brother, his wife, and their two children. Max
was a street peddler. Annie earned extra cash selling advertising
for Boston newspapers. Though she was bright, she lacked any
formal education.

Born in Riga, Latvia, in 1870, she immigrated with her family to Boston as a young girl. In 1887, after the death of both
parents, she and her siblings became orphans. The next year, at
age 18, Annie married Max and soon bore her first child.

"I didn't want to spend my life at home with a baby under my
apron every year," Annie later wrote. She wanted more from

life, and the prospect of a grand adventure was too much to refuse. Practically every day there were news reports of a man or woman starting off on some improbable escapade. These stories were closely followed by avid readers. Adventurers were the celebrities of the day.

Although people were rarely critical of a father or unmarried woman who embarked on a long adventure, a mother of young children doing the same would likely be judged harshly for abandoning her parenting duties. During this era—when women were demanding the right to vote, the right to higher education, and equal rights in marriage—the bicycle became a symbol of freedom. On two wheels a woman had more freedom to travel. As an energetic, intelligent, young Jewish immigrant, Annie saw an opportunity to use the bicycle as a means to achieve the fame, fortune, and freedom she craved. Cleverly she devised a plan to earn money for her family by capitalizing on the public's interest in bicycles, adventure, and women's rights. To succeed she would no longer be Annie Kopchovsky, a Jewish mother of three, but an unmarried woman named Annie Londonderry. In this new role she would capture the interest of the press and public by making the first attempt by a woman to cycle around the planet.

Hours before her scheduled departure, hundreds of well-wishers, including suffragists, friends, family, and other curious citizens, gathered to cheer Annie on her way. The head of the local chapter of the Woman's Christian Temperance Union declared to the crowd that women should have the same opportunities as men and expressed hope that Annie would set a fine example for women wherever she went. Annie explained that she was attempting her round-the-world ride to settle a wager between two wealthy men. If she returned within 15 months and earned $5,000 along the way, she would be awarded a prize of $10,000. She was not allowed to accept contributions and could earn money only by selling souvenirs or advertising, such as the $100 paid by Lithia Water Company. Annie then declared she was off to circle the world and pedaled away to the sound of cheers. One newspaper story reported that she "sailed away like a kite down Beacon Street."

After the grand send-off, Annie delayed her departure for two days to have official photographs taken. Finally, on June 27, she started pedaling south to New York. After a few miles the smooth, paved city roads gave way to rough country lanes. By nighttime she reached Providence, Rhode Island, where she spent the night. Covering a distance of more than 50 miles on her first day of cycling was impressive for an inexperienced cyclist and was proof of Annie's natural athletic ability. The question remained whether she had the endurance to go thousands of miles farther. While in Providence, she earned $50, plus money for her lodging, by lecturing and selling candy. Two days later she told a reporter from the *New York Herald* that she would pay for her way by selling photos, autographs, and lecturing, and that she had studied medicine for two years. This was the first

Annie, wearing "proper clothes" for pedaling her new Columbia bicycle.
Courtesy of Peter Zheutlin

of many newspaper interviews in which Annie freely invented "Annie Londonderry's" personal history.

After such a good start, Annie was stalled in New York, where she stayed with friends and sewed a new, improved riding outfit. This lighter dress had a comfortable bloused waist that could be pinned up when riding fast. To this she added a new cap and rubber-soled shoes. Her corset, which women were expected to wear, made riding difficult. It limited her movement and restricted her breathing, so she discarded it. Annie looked and felt like a new woman in her new, improved bicycle costume.

In an interview with a New York newspaper, she was asked if she was concerned about being attacked by tramps. Annie replied boldly that she carried a loaded pistol and therefore had no worries. In such interviews Annie played the role of a tough, self-assured woman who was prepared for any challenge. It was therefore no surprise that on July 28 a crowd of hundreds gathered to cheer as she cycled off for Chicago. It was a scorching hot day, and local male bicyclists snidely doubted that she would make it past the outskirts of the city, but Annie left New York City far behind as she rolled north to Albany. Day after day she cycled, over smooth and rugged roads, in sunshine and rainstorms, and each day she grew stronger. By September 24, when she wheeled into Chicago, she had traveled almost 1,000 miles.

In Chicago, Annie started to have doubts about reaching her goal. Ahead was the long ride through the Midwest and then across mountains to the Pacific Coast. Her success was no longer simply a private matter, for now she was a symbol to other women around the country. Annie didn't want to disappoint her supporters. Fortunately, before she abandoned all hope, Chicago's Sterling Cycle renewed her faith by offering her a 26-pound men's bike frame and an advertising contract.

Then the manufacturer of the tires for Sterling bicycles also offered her a contract. Now Annie had two more banners to fly from her bike and the courage to get back on the road, but she had changed her route. Incongruously, she decided to reverse direction, return to New York, and from there, board a ship to France. On October 14, when she pedaled away from Chicago, she was wearing bloomers. These long baggy pants with a narrow cuff at the ankle were normally worn under skirts and were a much more comfortable option for a woman riding a man's bike. Yet when asked by a reporter at the start of her trip why she wasn't wearing bloomers Annie had replied, "Although I'm cheek enough to go around the world, I've not enough cheek for that."

So with more cheek and stronger muscles, Annie cycled east. Along the way she was joined for short distances by other cyclists who had read about her and was hosted by cycling enthusiasts. As she stayed at small-town hotels, crowds gathered to stare at both her outfit and bike. Upon reaching Buffalo, New York, her next outfit garnered even more attention. Annie purchased a pair of boys' pants and shortened them to reach

Annie's bloomers and the Sterling bike were an improvement.
Courtesy of Peter Zheutlin

her mid-calf. She wore these "knickerbockers" with black stockings, gaiters, a tweed vest and jacket, and a blue yachting cap atop her head.

Bystanders were perplexed, wondering if the bicycle rider coming toward them was a woman or a man. Only on closer inspection did her "shapely form" solve the mystery. Annie arrived in New York City just in time to board the ship to Europe. On board she delighted in being the center of attention. She told tales of her adventure to the socialites and royalty who she met on board, pedaled her bike around the deck, and pocketed money earned from lecturing.

In Paris, Annie was offered lodging with a Sterling Cycle agent and his wife. There, news reporters showered her with adoration. Bicycles were as popular in France as they were in America, and Paris was ready for a cheeky American adventuress. One journalist wrote that despite her petite size she appeared to be made of only muscles and abounded with energy. It was the dead of winter and Paris was fascinating, but Annie had a schedule to keep. Six months had passed since the start of her trip, so she began cycling south to the port city of Marseille. Attached to her jacket she wore a piece of cloth with a message in French asking people to please show her the way. Along the route, she was escorted by other cyclists and cheered by small crowds. The weather was cold and snowy. The roads were muddy, but Annie pedaled onward. After days of frigid temperatures Annie felt fatigued but was buoyed on her arrival in Marseille, with its welcoming citizens and merchants eager to help her raise more funds.

On January 20, 1895, as Annie departed for Egypt on the *Sydney*, enthusiastic supporters stood on the pier to see her off. Now she was traveling more "with" her bike than "on" it. In Colombo, Ceylon, (present-day Sri Lanka) she took a "30-mile

There was plenty of publicity for the daring Miss Londonderry.
Courtesy of Peter Zheutlin

MISS LONDONDERRY IN DENVER.

The Brave Little Woman Is In the Best of Health, and Says She Is Enjoying Her Tour Immensely.

COLORADO ROADS IDEAL FOR CYCLING.

Miss Londonderry left Boston last spring for a trip around the world on a wheel. It was a great and hazardous undertaking for a girl; but she possessed the courage, and will win her wager.

Miss Londonderry, before leaving this country, contracted with the

Londonderry Lithia Springs Water Company,

of Nashua, N. H., to use the name "Londonderry" on her journey, and to her great surprise the people of every country she visited were familiar with the name as being connected with the celebrated Londonderry Lithia Water. Thousands of people spoke of the excellency of this wonderful water.

Miss Londonderry has been highly entertained by wheelmen all through her journey. A large delegation of Denver cyclists escorted her into Denver from Colorado Springs. She will remain in the city a few days before taking up her journey eastward.

spin" around the city with members of the local bike club. In mid-February when the ship made port in Singapore, she found herself accused as a fake by the local paper. It claimed that her passage via ship from France to Singapore made her round-the-world cycle trip much too easy. Annie chose to ignore this criticism. At each port Annie took time to raise funds, but she had few opportunities for cycling. Despite stories she later told about side journeys to Korea and Siberia, she was not in Japan long enough before her next voyage to San Francisco to have made these trips. During her lectures Annie always wove a good tale full of drama and detail, and the audience gobbled up every word.

Following her arrival in San Francisco at the end of March 1895, Annie promptly set off on the final leg of her journey. Accompanied by another cyclist, she wheeled her way toward Los Angeles. As she traveled across the southwest, much of it desert, she suffered accidents, extreme heat, and steep ascents. She gave racing demonstrations and added more advertising banners, until she eventually had more than 50 flags fluttering from her bike and clothes. In town after town she added to her coffers, selling souvenirs and promoting local merchants. In El Paso, Texas, the famous outlaw John Wesley Hardin attended one of her lectures to establish an alibi while one of his gang was "murdered by an enemy." In Iowa she broke her wrist, but she kept moving. On September 12, Annie pedaled precariously into Chicago with one arm in a cast. With the weather continuing to grow cooler, Annie cycled eastward. Each day her muscles grew stronger, and the distance to the finish line grew shorter. Finally she arrived back in Boston exactly 15 months after the start of her long journey. Annie hadn't pedaled over as much land as many had expected her to, but nonetheless her journey was a great accomplishment. She had been in the news for more than a year and proved herself to be an entertaining conversationalist and clever promoter. Two Yiddish words best describe her character: with chutzpah (audacity) and moxie (determination), Annie had accomplished her round-the-world journey.

Helga Estby

THE LONG WALK ACROSS AMERICA

> *"We were told at the start we would never make the trip, but we are confident of getting through successfully."*
> —*Helga Estby*

In 1984, professor Linda Lawrence Hunt read an essay that an eighth-grade student had entered in the Washington State History Day Contest. It was titled "Grandma Walks from Coast to Coast." Doug Bahr's essay recounted the story of his great-great-grandmother Helga Estby and her daughter Clara's long walk across America in 1896. Intrigued, Linda began searching for more information about Helga and Clara. Almost 20 years later, she published *Bold Spirit*, the tale of their long-forgotten adventure.

In the last decade of the 19th century, society expected women to be docile and let men make the important family decisions. Most men thought the ideal woman was a prim and proper lady who refrained from rigorous exercise and yearned to be a dutiful wife and mother. Many women had no choice to be otherwise. Across America women labored on family farms

Helga and Clara Estby dressed
in fine silk before their
journey.
Courtesy of Carole Estby Dagg

as well as in factories. Living a rough life to help support their families was their only option. As an immigrant farmer's wife, Helga Estby did her share of hard labor.

Helga Estby was born Helga Avilda Ida Marie Johanssen in Christiania, Norway, on May 30, 1860. Her father died when she was two years old, and her mother soon remarried. In 1871, she moved with her family to Michigan. By the age of 11, she had already been taught that serving a husband and family was her life's task. At 16 she married Ole Estby, a Norwegian immigrant like she was. She soon gave birth to her first child, and from that moment until 20 years later, when she was the mother of six children, Helga remained a truly devoted wife and mother. During those years she toiled alongside Ole as they homesteaded on the treeless, windswept Minnesota prairie.

Life was far from easy. She lost her second child, Ole Junior, but during the following few years gave birth to five more. Besides caring for six children, she cleaned the house and cooked. She made soap, candles, and butter. She also assisted her husband on the farm, planting, weeding, and harvesting crops. Years of constant hard work made Helga a strong woman. Year after year, she and Ole faced one challenge after another, from severe snowstorms to epidemics. They endured prairie fires and powerful thunderstorms that ravaged their homestead with high winds, heavy rains, hail, lightning, and tornadoes. After years struggling to make a decent life for their family, she and Ole finally decided that farming on the prairie was just too difficult to continue.

Seeking an easier life, they packed up and moved to Spokane, Washington. Life for the family improved until one night when Helga was walking home. Workers had neglected to place a safety barrier around a construction site, and Helga tripped on debris. She was so badly injured by her fall that she was unable to care for her family. She sued the city for carelessness, and after two trials she was finally awarded enough funds to pay for surgery. Meanwhile, crime was increasing in their neighborhood in Spokane. She and Ole grew concerned for the safety of their children and decided to move. They purchased a farm in Rock Creek Valley, 28 miles south of the city. Together Ole and Helga built a house and barn. With the help of their older children they cleared fields, planted orchards, and started a garden. Life was better, but hard times came again in 1893. During that year's financial panic, many banks closed, prices for crops plummeted, and jobs became scarce. After Ole had an accident, he was no longer able to do hard physical labor, and they had to take out a loan. Like many other farm families, they were now in danger of losing the farm to the bank. As if things weren't bad enough, in January 1896, their 12-year-old son, Henry, died from a weak heart.

In the midst of these family troubles, Helga received a strange offer from a "wealthy woman" in New York, who knew friends of Helga and Ole's. She offered to award Helga and her oldest daughter, Clara, $10,000 if they walked across America. It was an offer that came with many provisions. On the trek Helga and Clara were required to wear bicycle dresses as advertisement for this new type of apparel. They would have to pay their own way by earning money along the way for food and other necessities. They would also have to visit the governor of each state through which they passed and collect his signature. Most important, they had to reach New York in exactly seven months.

With Ole unable to support the family, Helga felt that she had to take this opportunity to earn the $10,000. She saw it as the only way to save the farm. Helga's family and neighbors feared for her safety. Many believed it would be irresponsible for her to leave her husband and other children. Helga, however, was confident that her oldest children could competently care for the younger ones.

On May 4, 1896, Helga and Clara set off wearing long dresses and carrying pistols, a homemade pepper spray device, and a letter of introduction from the mayor of Spokane. Helga believed that by simply focusing on placing one foot in front of the other, she and Clara could complete the long walk across America. To avoid getting lost, they decided to follow the railroad tracks.

For the first 10 days, they were soaked by rain and sleet. When they walked into a small village of mainly Norwegian residents, they looked forward to a warm welcome; instead they were shunned as scandalous vagrants. The townspeople refused to give them food or shelter.

As they trod on, mile after mile, both Clara and Helga became stronger and stronger. In southern Washington their route took them across Blue Mountains, which were still partly covered in snow. It was a cold crossing—they lacked blankets, boots, and food—but onward they trudged, eventually reaching the other side. Shortly afterward, when a tramp attempted to attack them, Helga whipped out her revolver and without any hesitation fired a warning shot.

On May 24, they walked into Baker City, Oregon, where a reporter described them as revolver toting, weather beaten, and sun brown. He quoted Helga as saying the trek had "given both [herself] and [her] daughter appetites like bears."

Even though Helga and Clara experienced only three days of decent weather during their first month of walking, they averaged 27 miles per day. When they strode into Boise, Idaho, on June 4 the citizens were in the midst of preparing for the flooding of the Snake River. Despite the chaos, Helga and Clara managed to meet Idaho's governor, who gladly added his signature to the letter of introduction. Before departing they cooked, cleaned, and sold pictures of themselves to replenish their travel money.

On the way south from Boise, Helga and Clara left the railroad tracks in hopes of making the route shorter. This turned out to be a big mistake. For the next three days they were lost in vast lava beds, where they became more hungry and exhausted each day. They might have perished there if they had not spotted the headlight of a nearby train. With overwhelming relief they were able to get back on track again. From there to Salt Lake City, Utah, Helga and Clara crossed miles of hot, dry land without any sign of other humans. They welcomed the sight of the first Mormon settlement they came to, because it meant that from that point on they would be able procure food and find lodging.

In Salt Lake City the governor of Utah added his name to the letter. Helga and Clara replaced their long skirts that had hems almost touching the ground with the more comfortable ankle-length bicycle skirts. This fashion, preferred by progressive women, was less restrictive to their moments and was an added comfort as they continued east to the Wyoming border.

From Evanston, Wyoming, the railroad tracks traversed a vast, high, dry, sagebrush-covered plateau. On these high, lonely plains they encountered more cattle than people and

Helga and Clara wearing their daring, short-hemmed bicycle dresses.
Courtesy of Carole Estby Dagg

had little shelter from strong, dusty winds that buffeted them each day. Some days they had to go without a meal or a shelter for the night. After their arrival in Laramie, Wyoming, in late August a reporter wrote, "They had been lost in forests, had adventures with mountain lions, but they trudged on in their short gray suits and came up smiling." Railroad workers who read about Helga and Clara's trek began leaving jugs of water by the tracks for them to drink as they trekked through sweltering, arid areas.

In Greeley, Colorado, Helga and Clara purchased new shoes to replace their worn ones. In the bustling city of Denver the governor of Colorado added his signature to the others. When Clara injured her ankle they had to rest for 10 days while she recovered. Helga was anxious to get back on the journey in order to meet the deadline, but Clara was growing weary of the arduous march.

The farther they walked, the more known they became. In Lincoln, Nebraska, Helga and Clara stopped by at the home of Congressman William Jennings Bryan. As the Democratic candidate for president, he was traveling the country. At each stop he gave a speech criticizing the power of the Wall Street banks and wealthy robber barons who he said were getting only richer as people like Ole and Helga grew poorer. Fortunately, his wife, Mary, was home and graciously invited Helga and Clara to dinner, purchased photographs, and signed their letter. As they tromped into Iowa in early October, temperatures were still warm. On October 17 when they arrived in Des Moines, they paused to earn some money to buy new shoes and mackintosh raincoats, because the weather had now turned cold and wet. With the signature of Iowa's governor in hand, Helga and Clara continued onward to Chicago. Realizing that the cinders along the railroad tracks had been quickly destroying their shoes, they started walking along the dirt roads bordering the railway whenever possible. As they marched eastward from Chicago, the weather turned frigid. William McKinley, the Republican presidential candidate, warmly welcomed them at his home in Canton, Ohio, and scribbled his signature on their letter.

Once more, this time in western Pennsylvania, Helga and Clara had to draw out their revolvers to dissuade two men from attacking them. Each day New York grew closer. At last on December 23, 1896, after walking more than 4,600 miles and wearing out 32 pairs of shoes, they stepped into the offices of the *New York World* newspaper.

New York newspapers heralded the story of Helga and Clara's amazing adventure. Other papers around the nation published reports. The Christmas Eve edition of Spokane newspapers even announced their safe arrival. That same day Helga and Clara received the devastating news that the mysterious woman who had offered the $10,000 had gone back on her word. She simply refused to pay them, and now, after having completed their remarkable feat, Clara and Helga were without any money or even a place to sleep in America's biggest city. They had to somehow find a way to earn money for train fare home. That winter and spring as both Helga and Clara toiled away accumulating travel funds, a tragedy had occurred back on the farm. One of Ole and Helga's daughters, Bertha, had died from diphtheria, and then four days later their son Johnny perished from the same illness. Stranded in New York, Helga and Clara were overcome with grief. Their luck turned in May, when a wealthy railroad magnate who had heard of their plight generously provided free fare to Chicago. From there Helga and Clara had to walk to Minneapolis, Minnesota, where the newspapers wrote detailed stories about the mother and daughter's remarkable trek across America. Carrying copies of these stories, Helga and Clara finally made it home to their suffering family.

There wasn't any hero's welcome, only blame and anger for Helga's absence. She was spurned by her neighbors and resented by her remaining children for her absence. The story of Helga and Clara's journey was silenced. For the remaining 45 years of her life, Helga never mentioned the trip. Only in later years after Ole had passed away and she was caring for her granddaughter Thelma did Helga start writing about her walk across America. She asked Thelma to tell her story one day but never told her granddaughter about the trek. After Helga died, her daughters Ida and Lillian found the manuscript and burned it. When Helga's daughter-in-law Margaret discovered two newspaper clippings about the walk, she kept them hidden from her husband and the rest of the family, fearing they would destroy them. Years later she gave them to Thelma, who, at last, was able to share Grandmother Helga's story. And it was her grandson Doug's retelling of the tale that brought Clara and Helga the recognition they deserved for their remarkable walk and tragic betrayal by an unscrupulous mystery woman.

Freya Stark

A FASHIONABLE NOMAD

> *"The wise man sits by the river, but the fool gets across bare-foot."* —*Arab proverb*

In 1928, Freya Stark and her friend Venetia quietly laughed in the washroom of a French fort in a remote part of Syria. They didn't have much time to invent an excuse for being in this forbidden region, where the French army had been trying to quell a rebellion by the local population against French colonial rule.

Before departing from Damascus, the Western European women had been informed about the travel ban in this zone, but with her typical disregard for rules, Freya ignored these warnings. Her mind was set on visiting the Mountain of the Druze to learn more about the mysterious Druze people. The Druze, an ancient religious sect, had broken away from the main branch of Islam centuries ago. During the Crusades they were some of the fiercest soldiers to fight the invaders from Great Britain and France.

Freya's old friend Venetia was reluctant to accompany her, until Freya convinced her that it would be easy to evade French army patrols. She also allayed Venetia's fears of entering Druze territory, despite the reputation the Druze had of attacking foreigners. Riding on donkeys, the two women followed behind their Druze guide, Najim, farther and farther south into the desert. Each day they encountered villagers, most of whom had never seen a foreigner, much less two foreign women. At each village they were graciously invited to share a meal and stay the night. Stopping at watering holes was risky due to the possibility of being attacked by Bedouin raiders.

As they finally arrived at the foot of the Mountain of the Druze, word of their journey had reached some French soldiers, who came looking for them and "invited" them to be guests at the French garrison. Though not technically arrested, Freya and Venetia were prevented from continuing their journey. To get out of this jam Freya had to use all her skills. She flirted, joked, and pestered the fort's commander until he was convinced the women were just harmless tourists. He gave them a letter of introduction to Sheikh Ahmed El Hajari, the high priest of the Druze, and then let them go on their way.

Far from being regarded as a threat, Venetia and Freya were treated as honored guests after their arrival in the sheikh's village. The sheikh was very interested in Venetia's stories about her travels in India, especially her descriptions of Hinduism and Buddhism. On hearing that Freya and Venetia had been "prisoners" of the French, the Druze villagers shared many heartbreaking stories about French brutality, including arrests and executions of Druze who revolted against the French takeover of their land.

For Freya, this first adventure felt like a great success. After years of studying Arabic she had made use of it to connect with and learn about the people of the desert. Her genuine interest and empathy set her apart from many other European travelers who routinely acted superior to people from other cultures. Using her wit and charm she had been able to overcome problems with the colonial authorities.

Freya wrote an article about her visit with the Druze and their problems with the French. To her delight, it not only was accepted for publication but also received praise. To avoid difficulties with the French in case she ever returned to Syria, Freya used the pen name Tharaya. It was the first of many written accounts that would be published and gain her fame.

From the start, Freya's life was one of travel. Thirty-five years earlier in 1892, she had been born prematurely during her mother's visit with a friend in Basingstoke, Great Britain. By the time she was four years old and her family had settled in Great Britain, Freya had already lived in numerous homes in France and Italy. Freya became multilingual, learning German from her grandmother, as well as French and English from her parents.

One day, young Freya marched out the front gate with a toothbrush and a penny in her pocket and headed for a "life at sea." The farther she walked, the bigger her journey seemed, and just as she was beginning to feel lonely, the postman took her by the hand and led her home. Years later she wrote that this initial "moment of emancipation still holds delight, of the world coming to meet you like a wave."

During these early years, there were frequent visits to see her grandmother in Genoa on the Italian coast and to visit Herbert Young, her parents' good friend, at his home in Asolo near the Italian Alps. Her family soon settled in a home in the village of Chagford, Great Britain, on the edge of the wild and windy Dartmoor. Across this open land she trekked with her father and younger sister, Vera. Her father, Robert, encouraged both her and Vera to be brave and curious. Like her father, Freya also loved to read. At age nine, after reading *One Thousand*

and One Nights (Arabian Nights), Freya became intrigued by the Middle East.

Through example, her mother, Flora, taught Freya to be charming, witty, and strong willed. Although Flora was extremely social, Robert enjoyed the peace and quiet of the moorland. As the years passed, her parents grew apart. When Freya was 10 years old, she departed with her mother and sister on yet another voyage to Italy. It seemed to Freya that they were going on vacation; she didn't know until later that her mother had no plans to return to Great Britain and her husband. Flora Stark had made plans to comanage a carpet factory with a young Italian count, Mario di Roascio, in the small town of Dronero, in the northwest corner of Italy.

Freya missed her father and the moors; she resented the hours her mother spent away from home managing the factory. She soon detested the count. Books and long walks in the hills became her refuge.

Then at age 13, an accident occurred that would physically and emotionally mar Freya for life. On a visit to the factory, her long hair became entangled in some machinery. As she was swung about, her feet were battered against a column. By the time the count finally wrenched her free, part of her scalp and a piece of one ear had been torn off. The pain was agonizing. Doctors were concerned that she might not survive her injuries and immediately performed an operation that kept her alive. It took a four-month stay in the hospital to recover. Though this ordeal taught Freya endurance, she would forever feel self-conscious about her appearance. Throughout her life she hid her scars beneath fashionable scarves and hats.

The only formal schooling she and Vera received was French lessons from nuns at the nearby convent. In spite of the hours she had to devote to household chores and later office

Freya Stark, wearing one of her
trademark fashionable hats.
Image Works

work at the factory, Freya
read book after book. She
taught herself math and
Latin. At the age of 20, she
had little problem passing
the entrance exam at the
University of London, where
she enrolled as a student. Despite
never having attended school, Freya
excelled, and professors took notice of her sharp mind and talent
for learning new languages. Her favorite, Professor Ker, encouraged her study of language. During vacations he led Freya and
fellow students on hiking and climbing trips. On a trip in the
Italian Alps he taught her how to use a rope and other climbing
gear to ascend peaks. Many years later, using these skills, Freya
became the second woman to climb Monte Rosa, the second
highest mountain in the Alps, via the treacherous route on the
Italian side of the peak.

With the start of World War I came major changes. When
classes were suspended, Freya decided to become a nurse.
Toward the end of the war she served with a British ambu-
lance corps and treated injured soldiers close to the battlefield
in northern Italy. Seeing so many young men die gave Freya the
determination to be more in charge of her destiny. After the war
she returned home and once more found herself taking care of
her mother. She felt trapped—her response was to begin learning Arabic. This mystified her mother, but beyond the joy of

discovering a new language, Freya sensed it would lead to new opportunities in her future. That moment came in the spring of 1928, when Freya departed for Beirut, Lebanon, with the goal of becoming fluent in Arabic. There she found a teacher to give her Arabic lessons and found lodging in a village on the outskirts of the city. As she explored small hamlets high in the pine forests, she practiced her Arabic with peasants and delighted in experiencing their culture. English citizens living in Beirut, who amused themselves with tea and lawn parties, were perplexed and shocked. They couldn't understand her desire to mingle with the "natives." Rather than joining her compatriots, Freya immersed herself in her fascinating surroundings and thirsted for adventure.

Later that year, after her journey to Mountain of the Druze with Venetia, she was anxious to return to Italy to see her family. No sooner had she returned home than she remembered all too clearly how she had felt caged by obligations. She now set her sights on her next exploration: learning more about an ancient, fanatic sect related to the Druze. Centuries ago this cult, known as the Assassins, had terrorized Islamic lands from Egypt to Persia by executing enemy leaders. The Crusaders had brought home horrific stories about them. Freya wondered whether any of the "Assassins" still existed in some remote region. She traveled to London to search for information at the British Museum. By the fall of 1929, Freya was back in the Middle East, residing in Baghdad, Iraq, in a home on the banks of the Tigris River. For the next several months she learned to speak Persian and worked on perfecting her Arabic.

In May 1930, Freya set off for the Alamut Valley in Iran, hundreds of miles to the north. Her research had revealed that the castle of Hassan-i-Sabbah had stood on the flanks of Alamut Mountain for six centuries before being destroyed by Mongol raiders. For the first 10 days of the trip she used all her skills of persuasion to urge her reluctant guides onward and upward through the rugged territory. Upon reaching Chala Pass they could finally see the Alamut country stretching out below them.

"This is the great moment when you see, however distant, the goal of your wandering," wrote Freya. As they descended into Chala Valley, Freya asked all the villagers she encountered for the names of any peaks and ridges within view. Bit by bit, she filled in the blank spots on her British government–created map. Within two days of turning up a side valley, they spied above them the towering castle rock. After some precarious scrambling high up the rocky ridge, she discovered the crumbling buttresses, walls, and tunnels that were all that remained of the Assassins' legendary stronghold.

Back in Baghdad, British intelligence officers were impressed by the corrections and additions she had made to their maps. Freya was thrilled at being respected as a capable explorer.

In August 1931, after a visit to her father, now living in British Columbia, Canada, Freya returned to the valley of the Assassins. This time she explored the previously unidentified castle at Lamiasar. The ruins sat high up a ravine that was too steep for mules to ascend. With all the authority she could summon, she ordered her unenthusiastic guide, Ismail, to continue with her on foot. The only visible route to the crumbling castle required them to ascend a slanting rock shelf. Again, Freya's mountaineering experience came in handy, and they reached the ruins without any mishap. Once there, Freya carefully jotted down her observations, sketched the layout, and described the condition of the ruins. She also took numerous photographs of architectural features. She was especially intrigued by the ingenious water system composed of a series of ditches for delivering water from the ridge above and giant cisterns for storing it.

To reach the castle Freya and her guide had passed through a valley swarming with mosquitoes. On the way back she collapsed near a small village. She was gravely sick with malarial fever and dysentery. By some miracle, Ismail located a vacationing doctor who saved her life. During her long convalescence, she stayed in the doctor's village until she was fit to return to Baghdad.

Later that year Freya continued her explorations in Iran. She even attempted to search for a cave with a hidden treasure that she had heard about from a young man from Luristan. Hoping to evade the Persian police, she entered the territory through a remote section, becoming the first European woman to visit Luristan. Unfortunately, the authorities eventually intercepted her. Playing innocent, she denied any interest in treasure hunting. Though she avoided arrest, the police insisted on escorting her back to the border, and Freya had to abandon her treasure hunt.

"The greatest and almost only comfort of being a woman is that one can always pretend to be more stupid than one is, and no one is surprised," states Freya in one of her books.

In 1933, Freya received exciting news. The Royal Geographic Society had awarded her the Back Memorial Grant for her explorations in Persia. This was an extremely rare honor for a woman explorer during her era. Her adventures in Persia were the subject of her first book, *Valleys of the Assassins*, which not only was critically acclaimed but also brought Freya fame. Now Freya was known for both her daring explorations and vivid writing.

In the following years, Freya wrote three books about her explorations of remote, ancient trade routes in southern Arabia where she rediscovered the site of Cana, an ancient Arabian port. During World War II she served the British government by cultivating the support of Middle Eastern peoples for the Allies.

She wed her friend, historian and diplomat Stewart Perowne, in 1947. However, the marriage wasn't meant to be, and they separated only five years later. During the next couple of decades, Freya traveled in Turkey and Syria, and finally at the age of 77 she went on her final trip to Afghanistan. Her experiences from all these years of travel have been the subjects of more than two dozen books, including a three-volume autobiography.

Freya finally retired in Asolo, Italy, to live in the house given to her by family friend Herbert Young. Two years later she was awarded the prestigious Founder's Medal of the Royal Geographical Society, and then in 1975 Queen Elizabeth knighted her Dame Freya Stark. Until she died at age 99, Freya worked at publishing her letters and collections of essays and entertained visitors with tales from her adventurous life which lasted nearly a century.

Alexandra David-Néel

SEEKING THE UNKNOWN

> *"I craved to go beyond the garden gate, to follow the road that passed it by, and to set out for the unknown."*
> —*Alexandra David-Néel*

A chill wind blew as Alexandra David-Néel and her friend Aphur Yongden sought a place to spend the night where they would be hidden from the monks at a nearby monastery. At that time, foreigners were forbidden to enter Tibet. For days, she and Yongden, a young monk, had been masquerading as Tibetan pilgrims in order to reach Lhasa undetected. No European woman had yet succeeded in entering Tibet's capital. They finally settled down for the night on the cold, rocky ground behind a boulder that was barely large enough to block the frigid breeze.

Throughout the journey, Alexandra constantly worried about being unmasked and wondered if they would soon be arrested. It had taken them so long to get this close to their goal. She was particularly concerned about being seen the following day—Yongden planned to buy food at the monastery, and she would have to wait for him by the roadside.

Alexandra David-Néel was born in Paris, France, on October 24, 1868. Her mother dressed young Alexandra in fine, lacy frocks. Though she appeared to be a "proper," dainty little girl, she didn't act like one. At age five she scampered off alone into the woods of Vincennes, where a guard found her at sundown and brought her to the police station. Alexandra protested when a policeman started to lead her home. The officer, ignoring her pleas, grasped her hand firmly and practically dragged her home. Feisty Alexandra clawed his hand with her fingernails and swore revenge at the adults who had interrupted her adventure.

When Alexandra was six years old, her family moved to Ixelles, Belgium. She was sent off to a strict Calvinist school, followed by further schooling at a Catholic convent, and during school vacations, Alexandra felt trapped in her parents' home with its daily routines and their lack of interest in the big, wide world. She dreamed of traveling the world and craved a life of adventure. She became intrigued by religions other than her father's rigid Protestant beliefs and her mother's rigid Catholicism.

At age 13, after reading about Buddhism, Alexandra purchased a porcelain figure of Buddha that she displayed in her bedroom next to a figurine of Christ. After she discovered the writings of ancient Greek philosopher Epictetus, she started sleeping on bare boards in imitation of the Greek stoics. She grew more headstrong and independent year by year. Before long she was taking off on brief adventures without her parents' knowledge.

Then at age 17, Alexandra, without a word of warning to her mother or father, boarded a train to Switzerland. Once there, she walked over Saint Gotthard Pass to Italy and arrived at Lake Maggiore penniless but elated. A year later Alexandra left once more without informing her parents. This time she traveled by bicycle, pedaling 600 miles south to the French Riviera and onward to Spain. She stopped at Mont Saint-Michel, France, on the way back. As she would on future journeys, she chose the longest route and slowest means of travel.

In 1889, following her 21st birthday, Alexandra moved back to Paris. "The City of Light" had changed a great deal since her early time there. In the spring of that year, the Eiffel Tower, a monument to the modern age, had just been completed. In Paris there were those considered the avante-garde—people with daring new ideas. Among these were artists called the Impressionists, who challenged traditional painting styles. There were theosophists, a group that promoted universal brotherhood; and anarchists, who advocated for more freedoms and rights. At first all this was overwhelming to Alexandra, but before long she immersed herself in this exciting new life. She sat in on classes in Asian languages at Sorbonne University. She spent hours studying ancient Hindu and Buddhist texts and art in the Guimet Museum. She even befriended anarchists and published a slim book of her own pro-anarchist ideas.

Alexandra's life of travel began after she received a small inheritance from her godmother. Using this money, she sailed off to India. While she was visiting the India-Nepal border, the sight of towering Himalayan peaks and the sound of Tibetan music deeply touched her. In the south near Madras, India, (now called Chennai), Alexandra studied yoga and Sanskrit, an ancient language of India. Finally she felt she was truly living the life she had dreamed of. When her money was spent, Alexandra returned to Europe. It would be some time before she found her path back to the Himalayas.

Back in Paris, Alexandra renewed her music and drama studies. In 1895 she was selected as lead female performer for a French acting troupe and traveled to French Indochina to present performances for French colonists. Alexandra was now a successful actress, but her singing roles damaged her voice and cut her career short. She next turned to writing novels but was unable to get any published.

At this point, Alexandra gave up hope of attaining great success as an actor or writer. She joined an acting troupe and performed in Athens, Greece, and then in Tunis, on the north coast of Africa. There the Muslim calls to prayer and the poetry of the Koran drew her attention, as did Philippe Néel, a handsome railroad engineer. They quickly fell in love and were married in 1904.

For the next seven years, Alexandra tried her best to be satisfied with the life of a housewife, but that wasn't her destiny. She still craved adventure, and Philippe, who knew this, suggested that she travel to India to continue her studies of Buddhism. He had no idea it would be 14 years before she came home. Alexandra was now 43 years old and suffered minor physical discomforts, as well as spells of depression. However, she still carried her youthful passions, and these spurred her on. After arriving in India in 1911, she received an invitation to the royal monastery of Sikkim. There she met the crown prince, Maharaj Kumar Sidkeong Tulku Namgyal. She immediately became both his close friend and "spiritual sister."

Alexandra's language skills and knowledge of Buddhism opened up doors to more adventures. In the Sidkeongs' company, Alexandra became the first European woman to be granted an audience with the 13th Dalai Lama of Tibet. When she stood at the northern border of Sikkim and got her first view of the high Tibetan tablelands, Alexandra was awed by the "calm solitudes" and sensed that she was finally seeing her true home. In 1914, as war was about to break out in Europe, Alexandra was the guest of Buddhist nuns in a remote monastery called the Sun Shrine, high in the Himalayas. That same year Buddhist monks in Sikkim honored her with the gift of holy robes designating her a lama.

The British who ruled India and the northern kingdoms of Sikkim and Bhutan were aware of her relationship with the crown prince, Sidkeong. Her influence with him made them nervous. When he died suddenly that year, despite his excellent health, many of his followers suspected he had been murdered for political reasons. Devastated by this loss, Alexandra set off into the high mountains in the company of a 16-year-old Sikkimese monk, Aphur Yongden. Two years before she had met the Gomchen of Lachen, and then she and Yongden planned on being his students. This learned hermit lama had lived without seeing anyone for five years in a remote cave at 12,000 feet above sea level; his only sustenance was scraps of food left by herdsmen. The Gomchen showed Alexandra to the small cave that would be her home and led Yongden to another one a short distance away. Both were a mile below the Gomchen's larger cavern. Each day Alexandra ascended the steep slope, even in deep snow, to sit for hours in silent meditation as the Gomchen conveyed his teachings. He did this, she wrote, by sending his thoughts to her mind through a process called telepathy. It was in this isolated and harsh setting that he introduced Alexandra to tantric Buddhism. During her final year of apprenticeship, Gomchen sensed she was ready for deeper learning and guided her in perfecting tumo breathing. This meditative technique allows the practitioner to raise his or her body temperature. A person skilled in tumo breathing can be warm even when naked in a snowstorm.

Alexandra proved to be an excellent student, but the Gomchen couldn't see her living the life of a hermit monk. He believed that she should be a sojourner, a person who finds and shares her wisdom as a traveler. To accomplish this Alexandra would have to travel to Tibet. This would not be an easy task. Foreigners were forbidden from entering this remote land by the British—the colonial rulers of India—as well as the government of Tibet. For Alexandra, obstacles like this only made the challenge more appealing.

"Any honest traveler has the right to walk as he chooses, all over the globe," wrote Alexandra David-Néel to express her disregard for borders.

In July 1916, Alexandra and Yongden departed for Shigatse, Tibet, at the invitation of the Panchen Lama. He was the abbot of the nearby monastic university of Tashilhunpo and Tibet's most important spiritual leader. Upon their arrival the lama took Alexandra on a tour of the many temples and palaces there and then granted her permission to study in his immense libraries. The lama's mother welcomed Alexandra into her home, and they quickly developed a close friendship. When she left in August, Alexandra carried two gifts from the Panchen Lama: an honorary doctorate and a lama's robe signifying her new status. Upon returning to Sikkim, the British authorities were infuriated by her illegal entry to Tibet and immediately deported her. Alexandra wondered if she would ever see Tibet again.

World War I was then raging in Europe, so returning there was out of the question. Instead Alexandra and Yongden traveled to Japan, where she met a Japanese monk who had managed to travel to Lhasa, the capital of Tibet, in the disguise of a Chinese monk. This gave her an idea about how she could return to the country that was her life's mission to explore. They traveled on to Korea, and then to Peking (now Beijing), China, and then joined the caravan of a wealthy Tibetan lama bound for Kumbum in northeastern Tibet. On the way they passed through a war-torn region ravaged by warlords battling for control. Eventually, in July 1918, after traveling mostly on foot for more than 1,500 miles, they reached their destination. She and Yongden spent two years translating ancient Tibetan texts amid the golden-roofed temples of the Kumbum monastery. With their minds still set on reaching Lhasa, they continued on their journey. After eight months of trekking, they reached a border of Tibet closer to Lhasa but were barred from entry.

Alexandra and Yongden were not ready to give up on their goal, no matter how long it took. They decided to retreat north to Jyekundo, a town high in the plains near the Great Desert of Grass that was ruled by a Chinese Muslim warlord. They became

stranded in the city due to a shortage of money, and heavy snows blocked any further travel. After being stalled for almost a year, they finally resumed their quest in August 1922. "People whose hearts are not strong and who cannot sufficiently master

Alexandra in her trekking clothes.
Archives Maison Alexandra David-Néel-Ville de Digne les-Bains

their nerves are wiser to avoid journeys of this kind," Alexandra
David-Néel later wrote of this trip.

The next segment of their journey was a long march of
2,000 miles, during which they traversed vast deserts, trudged
through soggy jungles, and passed through more battlefields. At
the end of eight months they were at last on the road to Dokar
Pass, their new entryway to Tibet.

Alexandra and Yongden stealthily crept toward the pass at
night, carrying all their possessions on their backs. Alexandra
was disguised as an old beggar woman. Hidden beneath her
clothing were her compass and a crude map of the region. During the trek to the pass they walked only at night and slept during the day, in places hidden from the eyes of other travelers.

"The majestic Kha Karpo towering in a clear sky lit by a full
moon did not appear to me that evening as the menacing guardian of an impassable frontier. It looked more like an affable deity,
standing at the threshold of a mystic land, ready to welcome and
protect the adventurous lover of Thibet," wrote Alexandra of
the high mountain that rose above them.

At Dokar Pass there were many small altars that had been
assembled by Tibetan pilgrims as offerings to the spirits. As
Alexandra and Yongden reached the top of the pass, they were
greeted by a strong gust. Snow swirled around the peaks above,
and darkness swiftly descended. While sleeping in a spot part-
way down the other side of the pass, Alexandra was awakened
by a soft sniffing sound. When she opened her eyes, a leopard
stood only a few feet away. She spoke to it gently before it quietly ambled away.

As they passed pilgrims or villagers during the following
days, Yongden was often asked to tell fortunes. At these times
Alexandra sat nearby with her face hidden from view. She once
more found her acting skills useful as she played the role of

Yongden's mother. She was fluent in Tibetan, having learned it while studying with the Gomchen. Locals who they encountered noticed that her accent and clothes were different. When they would ask about these things, she would reply that she was from the Desert of Grass or from the region of Kham. One day, she and Yongden found a fur-lined bonnet along the roadside. It was the same style as those worn by women in Kham. Though it was filthy, Alexandra knew it would be not only warm but also a useful disguise.

Besides the risk of Alexandra being recognized as a European, there were other perils. When they came to a river, the only way across was by being tied to an aerial cable and then pulled across. Alexandra wondered if she would survive as she and a Tibetan girl were being hauled over—she noticed that the strap that held them to the cable was frayed. If the strap broke, which seemed probable, they would be dropped onto the boulder-strewn river gorge far below. Luckily, the rope stayed intact.

Not long afterward, in late December, Alexandra and Yongden decided to follow a lesser-trod trail to the headwaters in the Peng Po Valley, even though they had been warned about armed bandits and the risk of being trapped by snowdrifts. The snow deepened as they approached the first pass. Slogging through the drifts was exhausting, and the higher they ascended, the more they gasped for air.

After they were over the 19,000-foot-high summit, they searched for a campsite and fuel. They found yak dung to burn, but the flint and dry moss they used to start fires were soaked. Their chance of surviving the night without the warmth of a fire was slim. Despite being out of practice, Alexandra succeeded in using tumo breathing to heat up her body to dry out the flint, steel, and moss that were tucked inside her dress. The fire and the shelter of their small tent kept them alive through the night, but their troubles were far from over.

The next night heavy snow collapsed their tent, and then Yongden badly sprained his ankle. On Christmas Eve they managed to locate an empty herder's cabin in which to spend the night. By the next day, Yongden was delirious with fever and they had consumed the last of their food. On Christmas Day they found another cabin. It appeared to be a fine gift until they discovered that it was occupied by bandits. Yongden cleverly informed them that his mother (Alexandra) was the wife of a powerful sorcerer, and the bandits kept their distance. Days later they reached a small hamlet, where the villagers were amazed that Alexandra and Yongden had survived the crossing of the high pass during the snowstorm. The rich turnip soup they were served, their first food in a week, was a welcome kindness.

They were now in Po country, a land no other European had ever seen. Though it was rumored to be a dangerous hideout for bandits, only once did they have to use their gun to fend off robbers. Day by day they neared Lhasa, and more and more people walked the road. Yongden and Alexandra were grateful to be able to blend with the throng of pilgrims and merchants. Early one morning Lhasa came into view and they had their first sight of the Potala, the palace of the ruler.

"Now we could discern the elegant outlines of its many golden roofs. They glittered in the blue sky; sparks seemed to fly from their sharp, upturned corners, as if the whole castle, the glory of Thibet, had been crowned in flames," wrote Alexandra.

Alexandra David-Néel had succeeding in becoming the first European woman to visit the remote and magical city. Starting from Kumbum three years earlier, she and Yongden had traveled more than 8,000 miles on their journey there. As exciting as this was, Alexandra had to keep her accomplishment a secret. This meant maintaining her disguise. Even though they could afford better, they found living quarters in a simple hut where they lived for the next two months side by side with some of the most impoverished Tibetans living in Lhasa. In her disguise Alexandra visited nearby monasteries and attended New Year festivities. It was only when she and Yongden departed that she could abandon her disguise as a beggar. She had been to Lhasa, so she didn't fear being deported. From then on, wearing the apparel of a lower middle-class woman, she and Yongden traveled with a servant and two horses. Alexandra was totally unaware that the English had known all along that she had made it to Lhasa and chose to leave her alone to avoid a fuss.

Alexandra would never return to Lhasa, but her book *The Journey to Lhasa*, as well as her other writings, revealed the hidden land to readers all over the world. Her rich, vivid descriptions of herders, villagers, monks, and high lamas brought Tibetans right to them. Her detailed chronicles were some of the first to reveal unique festivities and Buddhist ceremonies. Years later, the exiled 14th Dalai Lama wrote that the changes inflicted by the Chinese in Tibet since their invasion in the 1950s only made her accounts more important. They describe a country that no longer exists as it once did.

Alexandra eventually settled in France and was finally reunited with Philippe. Unable to overcome their differences, they dissolved their marriage but remained friends. She adopted Yongden as her son, and the two of them revisited Tibet in 1937. Philippe died in 1941, Yongden in 1955, and by the time Alexandra passed away in 1969 at the age of 100, her books were motivating a new generation of women to explore the Himalayas and inspiring Western poets and writers, such as Jack Kerouac and Allen Ginsberg, to learn about Buddhism.

Helen Thayer

FACING FEAR IN THE FAR NORTH

> *"One part of me wanted to go and run home, but an even big-ger part wanted to go to the pole and deal with whatever chal-lenges lay ahead, even polar bears."* —*Helen Thayer*

The night before embarking on the first solo ski trek to the magnetic North Pole, Helen Thayer couldn't stop worrying about being attacked by a polar bear. She had been carefully preparing for this journey for several days after arriving at Reso-lute Bay in the far north of Canada's Northwest Territories. She practiced setting her tent up and learned from local Inuit resi-dents how to drive away polar bears. The Inuit were alarmed by the thought of her traveling solo. They urged Helen to consider traveling in a safe fashion, such as snowmobile or dogsled. Sled dogs, for example, could repel bears. Though Helen was set on accomplishing her journey under her own power, she saw the wisdom in their advice to bring along a dog. One of the Inuit men sold her a big, black, 95-pound sled dog. For its whole life this dog had been member of a dogsled team. He had no name and had never, ever been treated as a pet. Helen named him

Charlie. Though she liked him right away, he seemed too easy-going to chase away a bear.

On March 29, 1988, Helen flew off on a small plane with Charlie as well as all her gear and food supplies. Her departure point was 67 miles north, at the Polaris mine. While mine employees were unloading their own supplies from the plane, a heavy crate fell on her carefully packed sled. Gear and other supplies that she had strapped onto the sled for easy access scattered all over the ground and then were haphazardly stuffed back on her sled. Helen decided to wait until the next morning, just before her departure, to repack the sled. That night she barely slept because she was so worried about running into polar bears. At breakfast the following morning she learned that a mama bear and two cubs had just been seen nearby her starting point; she instantly lost her appetite. As she attempted to reorganize the gear on her sled, well-meaning tourists insisted on helping her. Rather than telling them to go away, Helen simply zipped up the sled cover and decided to rearrange everything later. This was a big mistake.

Born Helen Nicholson in 1937 near Auckland, New Zealand, she grew up on a vast 10,000-acre sheep and cattle ranch. She was comfortable roaming the hills alone and spent hours exploring. Her father, Ray, who played soccer, and her mother, Margaret, a tennis player, encouraged physical exercise and her adventures. "They told me at a very early age, just because you're a girl doesn't mean to say you can't do what you want. Decide what you want to do, and do it right," Helen reported in an interview.

Her first ascent of a peak was at the age of nine, when she accompanied her parents up 8,200-foot-high Mount Egmont (now Taranaki). After standing atop the snow-capped volcano, Helen was more than ready to ascend another peak.

In 1953, Sir Edmund Hillary, a fellow New Zealander, and Tenzing Norgay of Nepal became the first people to summit Mount Everest, the world's highest peak. When Hillary visited her school to talk with students, Helen was so captivated that even years later Hillary remembered her. She decided she wanted to be a mountaineer just like he was. When Hillary explored the South Pole in 1958, Helen became determined to visit at least one of the poles. Over the next few years, this goal sat in the back of her mind. Meanwhile, she developed the physical and mental skills needed for such an adventure.

In 1962 Helen married Bill Thayer, a helicopter pilot. They moved to Washington State, where they owned and operated a dairy farm. Helen also became an exceptional athlete, especially in track-and-field sports. She was a champion discus thrower in the 1960s, and in 1975, at the age of 38, she won the US National Championship in luge, an extremely fast type of sledding. After that she went on to summit the highest peaks in New Zealand and North and South America, as well as the Pamirs in Tajikistan. While standing at the summit of the 23,405-foot-high Lenin Peak, Helen realized it was finally the time to attempt a polar journey. Over her years navigating with a compass through wild landscapes, Helen had developed a curiosity about the magnetic North Pole. Unlike the geographic North Pole, which is a point on the map, the magnetic North Pole is a region that shifts its location due to changes in the Earth's core. As her compass had always pointed north, so did Helen. Both her husband, Bill, and her parents supported her plans for her solo ski trek.

On March 30, 1988, Helen skied off toward the magnetic North Pole, pulling her seven-foot-long fiberglass sled loaded with 160 pounds of food, gear, and fuel. This was everything she would need for her month-long journey. Included in the gear was a rifle and orange flare pistol for protection against bears.

Helen and Charlie on their way to the magnetic North Pole.
Courtesy of Helen Thayer

At her side Charlie pulled his own sled packed with 85 pounds of dog food.

The temperature was −32°F. Helen stayed toasty enough while skiing, but she cooled off quickly after stopping. On her face she wore a neoprene mask and goggles to shield her face from the frigid air. Every two hours she made sure to down a cup of a hot, high-carbohydrate drink and munch a handful of high-fat snacks. At the same time she also fed Charlie a handful of dry dog food. Progress was slow due to Helen being on constant lookout for polar bears. Several times they crossed not only the tracks of the mother bear and her cubs but also those of a male bear.

Her route followed the coast of Bathurst Island, an uninhabited landmass larger than the state of Connecticut. The first evening Helen decided to set up camp at 6:00 PM because the temperature had dropped rapidly to −45°F. Her hands were frigid as she searched for items, such as her heavy mittens, which had been repacked haphazardly on the sled. By the time she located the mittens, her fingers were numb and white. To get blood to her now-protected fingers, she swung her arms around and around. As her fingers grew warmer a hot, searing pain replaced the numbness. She realized her fingers weren't frostbitten, but the pain was still agonizing. With her injured hands it was difficult to set up the tent. After neatly placing her cooking gear, clothing, journal, data book, and sleeping bag and pads in the tent, Helen discovered that she was unable to assemble the stove with her injured fingers. She had to eat her dinner cold and drink the last cup of water she would have until she could get the stove operating and melt some snow. This was not a good start to her 340-plus-mile trek.

As she would do each night, Helen radioed the innkeepers at Resolute Bay and reported her exact location, current weather conditions, and the miles traveled. She informed them that no bears had been sighted but didn't mention the condition of her hands.

The next morning Helen's fingers were worse. They were covered with blood blisters that made it excruciating to use them. To make matters worse, just after breakfast she heard Charlie make a deep, low growl. Not far away were a mama bear and two cubs. As the dog snarled viciously, Helen clipped him to a tie-down rope to prevent him from running after the bear. The mama bear slowly began plodding toward Helen. Despite Helen firing a warning shot with the rifle, the bear kept coming. Shooting a flare did nothing to halt the bear's advance. However, the combination of firing off a series of flares and Charlie's ferocious snarling finally deterred the bear. Followed by her cubs, she slowly lumbered away. Though Helen felt like a nervous wreck, she and Charlie had successfully scared away their first polar bear.

Later that day as they continued their journey, Helen used more flares to drive away two more bears. By 5:00 PM she was so worn out by these bear encounters that she stopped early to set up camp. They had traveled only three miles. The injuries to her hands made every activity so painful that Helen cried in despair. For the rest of her expedition Helen would have moments like this, and each time she had to turn her mind to thoughts of past accomplishments to help her believe in her ability to succeed. In the end the only thing her crying accomplished was to make her eyelids freeze together. Afterward she sat next to Charlie, who laid his head on her knee before falling asleep on her lap. Helen felt grateful for his devotion and realized she had to trust his ability to detect and drive away the bears.

During the next few days they journeyed through beautiful ice formations and glimpsed arctic foxes. Helen learned to navigate through areas of rough sea ice. The glare and her iced-over goggle lenses resulted in a lack of perspective in the vast white landscape, which made it difficult to judge the terrain that lay ahead. The extremely cold temperatures caused ice crystals to form between the outer shell of her coat; by the end of each day her coat became as constraining as a straightjacket. Each night in the tent she had to thaw out both her mask and jacket so she could use them the following day.

As they traveled through the ominously named Polar Bear Pass, a large male bear charged out from behind a small iceberg locked in the ice pack. As soon as Helen let Charlie loose, he dashed over to the bear, sinking his teeth into its back leg. As Charlie held on tight, he skillfully twisted away from the bear's snapping jaws. The bear ran off as soon as it dislodged Charlie, but Charlie kept up his attack until the bear was gone from sight.

Helen Thayer peeking out from her frozen ice mask.
Courtesy of Helen Thayer

Three days later a fierce storm blew in from the south. After first repelling another bear, Helen and Charlie climbed into the tent, where they stayed for three days, waiting for calmer weather. By now the blood blisters on Helen's hands had burst, and using them was more excruciating than ever. Added to this difficulty was the cracking of the sea ice beneath the tent. It was a relief when the wind died down enough for Helen and Charlie to pack up the gear and depart. Navigating through the fractured ice had to be done with the greatest of care. At times they had no choice but to cross over gaps—some of them three feet wide. Helen was well aware that falling into the frigid seawater would mean instant death. When at last they reached solid ground, she felt as if she had awakened from a terrible nightmare.

Travel during the next four days of clear weather was a vast improvement, but there were still more bears to drive away and more sections of thin ice to avoid. With the better conditions, they were able to trek longer and longer distances each day. Helen made up the days she had lost during the storm. After she made it to the northern tip of Bathurst Island, Helen got ready for the 70-mile journey across the sea ice to King Christian Island. She was now so close to the magnetic North Pole that her compass no longer functioned. In its place Helen used a chart that showed the exact time when the sun would be due south. Making use of this chart and a sundial, she was able to calculate the correct angle west of north that she had to follow. It took three long days of travel before they reached land. Helen then confirmed her location on King Christian Island with an experimental GPS instrument that she carried with her. The following day Helen skied to the northwest tip of the island from where she planned to head south to the area of the magnetic North Pole. On the way she and Charlie encountered a zone of thin ice plates, and Charlie resisted going with her. Out on the ice, a plate broke loose, tilted, and almost dumped them into the sea. Later Helen wondered if Charlie had sensed that the sheet of ice might tip. Day by day she was learning to trust the judgment and skill of this dog that had lived his whole life in the Arctic.

They started for the pole at 1:00 AM. By 4:00 PM they were only a couple of miles from the pole when Helen sighted a storm approaching from the south. When she realized just how fast and furiously it was advancing, she quickly anchored both sleds with ice screws. She was just about to pitch the tent when she sensed that it was too late. She pulled the zipper on the sled bag closed and was about to tighten a tie-down rope when the wind knocked her over. Creeping on hands and knees behind her sled, she then watched in horror as her gear and food began flying out of the sled bag. Without the tie-down rope to secure it, the zipper had blasted open. Luckily, Helen managed to shut the zipper before everything was lost.

When the wind paused, Helen realized that when she had been knocked down her face had been cut and her right eye was injured. Unable keep her eye open, she began to despair. From past experience she knew it wouldn't help at all to lose faith and told herself, "The Arctic has rammed everything down my throat from polar bears, to storms, to weird ice, and now this. I'll sit this storm out and make it."

During a lull in the storm, she was finally able stand up enough to erect the tent; she prayed that it would withstand the wind, which was roaring as loud as a jet engine. It wasn't until after the storm had blown out that Helen discovered all that was left of her food supply was a small bag of walnuts. There was barely enough fuel left to melt enough ice for a bottle of water per day. Several sacks of dog food had also been blown away. On half her normal ration of water and scarcely enough food, Helen would have to continue onward to the pickup point, where a plane would retrieve her. She had already been through a lot, but these next days would take all the emotional, spiritual, and physical strength she possessed.

Despite these troubles Helen was joyous the following day when she arrived at the pole. She had achieved her mission of becoming the first woman to reach the pole on a solo voyage. To document her accomplishment, she snapped photographs of herself and Charlie posing with the flags of the United States, Canada, and New Zealand. Helen had reached her goal, but now she had to get to the place where the plane was scheduled to pick her up. It took seven days to get there, during which Helen endured hunger, thirst, and limited sight. Despite the odds, fueled by faith and grit, Helen managed to reach the rendezvous point. From there she and Charlie were evacuated and returned

Helen and Charlie
reach their goal!
Courtesy of Helen Thayer

to the Polaris Mine. An explorer with less experience and determination would not have made it home, especially without a partner like Charlie.

Helen Thayer went on to walk across the Sahara and Gobi Deserts, kayak more than 2,000 miles on the Amazon River, and return for another Arctic journey with Charlie and her husband, Bill. Charlie became the star at school presentations where Helen talked to students about her adventures. He died in 2007 after a long and happy life. Helen said about her influence on children, "I want them to say, 'If she can do it, I can do it.'"

Kira Salak

DISCOVERIES IN TWO WORLDS

> *"I always needed to be gone. It was as a kid that the world I wanted and couldn't seem to find, lay elsewhere."* —Kira Salak

Kira Salak was traveling through Africa and had just reached the southern part of Malawi. The next country to the south was the war-torn nation of Mozambique, a former Portuguese colony. Factions had been fighting in the civil war for 15 years. Kira had heard tales of how soldiers, many of whom were children, had horribly tortured and mutilated civilians. But she was so determined to travel through Mozambique to reach the nation of Zimbabwe that she dismissed the danger of going there. With unexpected ease she obtained a visa to cross the border. She then persuaded a trucker named Jerry to give her a ride to Zimbabwe. He had warned Kira that his dilapidated truck might break down at any time, but Kira still wanted the ride. One of Jerry's truck-driving friends offered to follow behind to help out if needed.

As they departed Malawi, both trucks joined a caravan of other trucks. This was considered the safest way to cross the embattled Tete Corridor. Jerry and his friend told Kira tales of ambushes during which trucks were robbed and sometimes drivers were shot. Kira brushed aside these warnings. Not until she actually saw the wrecked vehicles, demolished houses, and disfigured civilians along the roadside did she begin to have doubts. By that time it was too late—and as forewarned, Jerry's truck broke down just a few miles short of the Zimbabwe border. The seriousness of this occurrence was magnified when a patrol of teenage soldiers stopped to inspect the truck. Upon seeing Kira, they ordered her out of the truck. Now Kira was truly terrified. She refused to come out and even resisted as the soldiers dragged her from the cab and threw her into their truck. She was hauled off to an empty building in the bush and told to sit on a bench while the soldiers proceeded to get drunk. Her pleas for release were not only ignored, but they may have encouraged the boys to taunt her by tossing plastic bottles and baobab pods at her. Kira knew she must escape before they summoned the courage to physically assault her. She waited for her chance, and it came soon. On the way back from the outdoor bathroom, Kira suddenly dashed out into the black night. She sprinted as she had years earlier during school races, quickly leaving the drunken soldiers behind. On and on she ran until she reached the border and met up with Jerry and his friend. She had survived physically unscathed, but the memory of this near-catastrophe would haunt her for years to come.

Kira Salak was born on September 4, 1971, in a suburb of Chicago, Illinois. As a six-year-old, she created her own adventure stories set in places such as the Andes Mountains or New Guinea. In these tales Kira was always the heroine, whether her character was an explorer, soldier, empress, or medicine woman. The heroine always possessed special skills, displayed extraordinary strength, and accomplished her mission, no matter how perilous. Kira discovered exotic settings for her tales as she leafed through the pages of *National Geographic* magazine or watched travel shows on PBS. Day after day during summer vacations Kira acted out these adventure dramas.

At school Kira was so shy that she kept to herself. She was afraid of saying something stupid, but being quiet didn't help; it only brought on teasing from her classmates. Kira did spend time with her older brother, Marc, who allowed her to tag along on his explorations of nearby fields and woods, but she didn't play with anyone her age. As Kira grew older, her parents worried about her lack of friends. They thought a new school might help her come out of her shell, so when Kira was 13, they sent her off to a boarding school in Wisconsin.

Strangely enough, Kira transformed into a different person shortly before the start of school. The track coach had discovered she was a talented runner and placed her on the team. Kira won race after race after race and was praised by her fellow students. Next she became a school hero for breaking the Wisconsin state record for the fastest mile by a female high school athlete. She was showered with attention by her coach, teachers, students, and her parents—and it terrified her. It felt like she had stepped onto a runaway train. Her natural talent as a runner had put her in a situation in which she was now expected to win. These expectations seemed like a trap. Her real dream was to be a writer, not a runner. Summoning all of her courage, Kira made the decision to quit running. When she told her parents of her passion for writing, they couldn't understand why she would want to quit the track team. And even worse, they couldn't understand why anyone would want to be a writer. To Kira it seemed as if she had let everyone down.

Once again, she reverted to being the quiet, invisible girl. In the depths of depression, she wondered how she would live her life. The answer came a few years later, when she was 19. The solution suddenly seemed so clear. It was time to abandon imaginary adventures for real ones. All she had to do was save her money, buy a plane ticket to an exotic place, and go somewhere where she could be whomever she wanted to be.

"Traveling could allow me to be reborn," Kira Salak later wrote.

Within a year she flew to Egypt. Finally the exotic scenery, the sounds, and the smells of a foreign land were not in her imagination but all around her. In this completely different world, she was both fascinated and afraid. For once she felt vibrantly alive. The following year, in 1992, Kira traveled around East Africa, where she had her terrifying experience with rebel soldiers.

Back home, Kira embarked on her path to become a writer. She entered Emerson College in Boston where she earned a BFA in writing, literature, and publishing. Next she enrolled in the writing program at the University of Arizona in Tucson and received an MFA in writing in 2004. While in a doctoral program in creative writing at the University of Missouri, Kira felt the need to travel once more and got permission to take time off from school. Since childhood, Kira had dreamed of trekking through the lush jungles of New Guinea and encountering isolated tribes.

Kira's goal was to become the first woman to travel across the island from the south coast to the northern shores. Her plan was to follow the Fly River to its headwaters, traverse the towering central mountain range, and descend from the upper reaches of the Sepik River to its outlet in the Bismarck Sea. This island, with its remarkable diversity of indigenous cultures and wide variety of plants and animals, would have many surprises for her.

Kira with a villager in Papua New Guinea.
Courtesy of Kira Salak

When she arrived in Port Moresby, Papua New Guinea's capital, she was shocked to discover that it was considered one of the world's most dangerous cities. She witnessed the city's residents huddling behind barbed-wire fences terrified about being attacked and robbed by hoodlums, known as rascals. This situation made Kira anxious to leave the city and start her journey in a wilder part of the island.

As soon as she could, she caught a flight to the town of Daru near the mouth of the Fly River. What Kira lacked in funds, experience, and knowledge to succeed in her expedition, she would need to make up for with her determination, physical strength, and good fortune. Right from the start she had problems with the boatman she hired to take her upriver in his motorized dugout canoe. After starting the journey he demanded more money than they had agreed upon. When she refused to pay more, he simply abandoned her in a small riverside village. Luckily there was an Australian miner fishing near the village, and he was willing to help. Using his boat's radio, he arranged for the company he worked for to send a helicopter to pick her up and drop her off upriver. The pilot deposited Kira in Kiunga, a village not far from the border of West Papua. From villagers she learned of a nearby refugee camp called Blackwater and arranged to be taken there. Her guides were refugee rebel soldiers fighting to free West Papua, a former Dutch colony that had been invaded 40 years earlier by the neighboring nation of Indonesia. Under Indonesian rule, tribal people had been forced off their land so that the forests could be logged. Other areas had been ravaged by the toxic waste from mining operations. Against great odds the rebel soldiers of the free Papua movement were attempting to reclaim their homes.

Kira traveled up the Sepik River in their convoy of two motorized dugout canoes. When she arrived at the camp she was welcomed with dancing and a feast. She interviewed the refugees and took notes detailing the atrocities committed against them by the Indonesians. She met with the mild-mannered Papuan minister who was the rebel leader, and he urged her to get word of his people's plight to readers in the United States. This material could have landed her in jail. Back in Kiunga, she mailed the notes to her family's home in Chicago.

Within a few days of arriving in Kiunga, she joined a Papuan man who was going to visit his sister, who lived in Hotmin, a small village across the steep mountains near the head of the Sepik River. They were guided by a shoeless elderly woman named Mila.

"The jungle folds us in its tangled innards as if we were traveling through the belly of some gigantic beast," Kira wrote of the journey. Heavy rains and knee-deep muck made the journey a difficult one for Kira. The air was as humid as a steam bath. It was constantly a struggle for her to keep up with Mila. To Kira, Mila seemed to walk effortlessly, even as she hacked brush with her machete. On the other hand, Mila found Kira's clumsiness amusing. Before long they were ascending a steep mountainside using roots and branches to haul their bodies upward.

At night, squadrons of voracious mosquitoes feasted on Kira's blood while Mila slept peacefully. By the time they had crossed the mountains, Kira's legs were bloody, swollen, and covered with cuts. Thorns were embedded in her shins. Though she was exhausted and felt like giving up, Kira remembered how during her track-and-field days she had summoned strength at the end of a tough race. These memories carried her onward.

Just before they reached the village, Kira was so fatigued she doubted she could go farther. Ahead was a thin, bouncy tree trunk that served as a bridge across a 30-foot-wide river. Kira was sure that she would fall, but using her last bit of strength she managed to make it step by step across the span. Upon reaching the village on the other side, she collapsed from heat exhaustion.

After resting for many days, Kira eventually regained enough strength to continue. She hoped to make it to a mission downriver, but to do so she had no choice but to hire an untrustworthy and possibly dangerous boatman. Going by the name of Mozart, with his scarred face and an empty eye socket, he looked like a comic book villain. With him were two equally scary companions. Kira feared she would be robbed or possibly murdered, so during the entire boat ride she kept hold of her machete. Mozart told her about killing two men with a knife. He asked her to hand over the machete, saying, "No can hurt you," but Kira refused to relinquish her weapon.

In the village where they stopped for the night, Kira had to share a hut with the men. It was a long night as cockroaches swarmed over Kira while she forced herself to stay alert and awake, ready to fend off an attack. When they arrived at the mission safely, she was only too glad to part ways with Mozart and his sidekicks. From there she caught a ride on a missionary plane farther downriver to the town of Ambunti. There she met an Australian traveler named Rob who wanted to float down the Sepik River to the sea. Kira thought it would be a great adventure and decided to join him. Aboard a makeshift raft composed of a bamboo platform strapped atop two dugout canoes, they traveled for several days until reaching a small town near the coast.

Kira had completed her first big journey despite many dangers. She had encountered incredible people along the way and viewed remarkable landscapes. This adventure and earlier ones became the subjects of her first book, *Four Corners*, published in 2001. An editor of *National Geographic Adventure* who read it was so impressed that he asked Kira to write for the magazine. Kira was now 31 years old, and besides being a rugged adventurer, she was writing for the magazine that had inspired so many imaginary adventures. The *New York Times* dubbed her "a real-life Lara Croft."

For the next few years, Kira went on assignments to chronicle her adventures in Rwanda, Libya, Burma, Borneo, and Uganda. When she traveled in Iran, she retraced the footsteps of pioneering explorer Freya Stark, who had investigated remote areas of Persia in the 1930s. In her second book, *The Cruelest Journey*, she wrote about her epic 600-mile kayak trip on the Niger River through Mali and celebrated the explorations of Scotsman Mungo Park, who was murdered during his second expedition in the region. Through day after day of fatiguing paddling and scorching temperatures, the Niger transformed in

Kira's thoughts from a waterway to a personality. It had become a "fickle parent," challenging her with storms and winds.

The drowning death of her brother, Marc, in Angola when Kira was 35 years old left her feeling shattered. Writing and traveling had been the tools Kira used to support herself emotionally, so writing her novel, *The White Mary*, enabled her to weather the loss of her only sibling.

In 2005, the National Geographic Society honored Kira with an Emerging Explorer Award. In writing about her encounters with people in less-visited regions, Kira had exposed injustices, such as slavery in Timbuktu and ethnic cleansing in West Papua. Like other bold women adventurers of the past, she had traveled solo and ignored other people's doubts about what she could do.

"When they say I can't accomplish a challenge, I just eat that up," said Kira, echoing the attitudes of many of the female explorers who preceded her. Unlike other women travelers of past times, as Kira explored she not only wrote about foreign lands but her own emotional experiences as well. She has revealed her discoveries in both her inner and outer worlds. For Kira, the acts of travel and describing her adventures have defined her life. And it is a life that inspires a sense of adventure in all of us.

Acknowledgments

In writing this book I received assistance from many generous people. I thank Beverly Wilgus for the use of her *carte de visite* of Martha Maxwell, Carole Estby Dagg for use of photos of Clara and Helga Estby, Doug Fesler for use of his photos of his wife Jill Fredston, Heather Jackson for use of the "frog queen" photo of her daughter Kate, Michigan State University for the use of a Pamela Rasmussen photo, Nikhil Devasar for use of his Pamela Rasmussen photo, Peter Zheutlin for Annie Londonderry images, Russell A. Potter for the use of a Hassan Cigarette trading card of Annie Smith Peck, Hannah Scialdone-Kimberley for help with locating photo of Annie Smith Peck, and the Bancroft Library, University of California Berkeley, for help with the Ynes Mexia photo.

In addition I owe thanks to David McClay, curator of the John Murray Archive at the National Library of Scotland for information on Isabella Bird, Linda Eade for research assistance for Ynes Mexia, and Lynn MacMichael for suggesting that I include Alexandra David-Néel in my book.

I especially want to thank Constanza Ceruti, Aparajita Datta, Jill Fredston, Kate Jackson, Lorie Karnath, Meg Lowman, Rosaly Lopes, Pamela Rasmussen, Kira Salak, Stephanie Schwabe, and

Edie Widder for taking time out of their gloriously full lives to answer questions, chat, and provide photographs.

And as always, many thanks to my wife, Lisa Rhudy.

Resources

66south.com

http://66south.com

This website about "passionate exploration" contains image pages of Alexandra David-Néel, Rosaly Lopes, Kira Salak, Freya Stark, Helen Thayer, and podcasts about Isabella Bird Bishop, Alexandra David-Néel, Rosaly Lopes, and Freya Stark, as well as oodles of information about other explorers.

American Alpine Club

http://americanalpineclub.org

303-384-0110

710 Tenth Street, Suite 100

Golden, CO 80401

The American Alpine Club was founded in 1902 to promote and preserve the climber's way of life. John Muir was the club's second president. Four women, including Annie Smith Peck, were among the club's founding members. In 2006, the AAC, in cooperation with the Mountain Institute, founded the Alpine Conservation Partnership, an organization dedicated to protecting and restoring the world's alpine environments.

American Association of University Women (AAUW)
www.aauw.org; connect@aauw.org
202-785-7700; 800-326-2289
1111 Sixteenth Street NW
Washington, DC 20036
Since its founding by prominent scientist Ellen Swallow Richards in 1881, the American Association of University Women has been supporting generations of young women in obtaining a college education through study, mentoring, and financial aid.

Annie Smith Peck: A Woman's Place Is at the Top
http://anniesmithpeck.org
This site was put together by researcher Hannah Scialdone-Kimberley and has rare photos of Annie Smith Peck and a concise time line of her life.

AVoCet: Avian Vocalizations Center
http://avocet.zoology.msu.edu
517-353-5428
20 Natural Science Building
East Lansing, MI 48824
Birds of the World was all Pamela Rasmussen had when she was a youngster. That book and occasional visits to the library helped answer many of her questions. Now, thanks to Pamela Rasmussen and her staff, you can visit this site to learn more about birds by listening to recordings of their songs.

Blue Holes Foundation
www.blueholes.org
Started by Stephanie Schwabe and Rob Palmer, this organization is dedicated to the scientific and physical exploration of water-filled caves within the Bahamas and related environments. You can view films of three different cave explorations: Stargate, Mermaid's Lair, and the Black Hole.

CanopyMeg

www.canopymeg.com

Meg Lowman's official website includes information about her work. It is chock-full of audio and video files which provide information on everything from protecting trees in Ethiopia to sloth and elephant conservation, and from a student belly-button diversity project to information about Treetops Camp in Elmira, New York.

Explorers Club

www.explorers.org

212-628-8383

46 East 70th Street

New York, NY 10021

The Explorers Club has supported explorers for more than 100 years. The club headquarters in New York City have served as a gathering place and a repository of journals, letters, maps, and artifacts from expeditions. Included in its illustrious membership are the first people to reach the North and South Poles, the summit of Mount Everest, and the surface of the moon. Lorie Karnath served as its second female president.

Helen Thayer

www.helenthayer.com

This site features photos of Helen Thayer's trips as well as videos and sample pages from her journals.

Isabella Bird at John Murray Archive in Scotland

http://digital.nls.uk/jma/who/bird

This site displays some of Isabella Bird Bishop's photographs, one of her letters, and her Korean passport, and it features a short film about her.

Kate Jackson

http://people.whitman.edu/~jacksok/CongoEN.html

Here you can find information and photographs of Kate Jackson's four herpetology expeditions in the Congo.

Kew Gardens Marianne North Gallery Online

www.kew.org/mng/gallery/index.html
Visit this site to view Marianne North's collection of paintings portraying plants from six continents.

National Outdoor Leadership School

www.nols.edu
800-710-6657
284 Lincoln Street
Lander, WY 82520-2848
Founded in 1965 by legendary mountaineer Paul Petzoldt, National Outdoor Leadership School (NOLS) takes students of all ages on remote wilderness expeditions and teaches them technical outdoor skills, leadership, and environmental ethics. Explorer Jill Fredston is an alumna, as are many other adventurous outdoorswomen.

Nature Research Center

http://naturalsciences.org/nature-research-center
919-707-9800
11 West Jones Street
Raleigh, NC 27601
The Nature Research Center is the kind of place Meg Lowman, its director, would have wanted to visit when she was young. Its goals are to bring research scientists and their work into the public eye, help demystify what can be an intimidating field of study, better prepare science educators and students, and inspire a new generation of young scientists. If you have a question about the natural world, you can send it to a naturalist from a form on the contact page.

ORCA (Ocean Research and Conservation Association)

www.teamorca.org/cfiles/home.cfm
772-467-1600
Duerr Laboratory for Marine Conservation
1420 Seaway Drive
Fort Piece, FL 34949
Co-founded by Edie Widder in 2005, ORCA tracks and analyzes aquatic ecosystems and species. The site lists internships for local

college and high school students, as well as opportunities to donate to or volunteer with the organization.

Outward Bound

www.outwardbound.org
866-467-7651
910 Jackson Street, Suite 150
Golden, CO 80401

The Outward Bound movement is based upon the principle of hands-on learning through outdoor adventure. Since 1961 Outward Bound has been teaching outdoor skills and team building to a wide variety of students, from at-risk youth to veterans from the wars in Iraq and Afghanistan.

Sierra Club Inner City Outings

www.sierraclub.org/ico
415-977-5568

Sierra Club Inner City Outings is a community outreach program that provides opportunities for urban youth and adults to explore, enjoy, and protect the natural world. The Sierra Club has 50 volunteer-run ICO groups spread throughout the United States. Every year, these groups conduct more than 800 outings that serve approximately 14,000 youth, helping these participants learn how to enjoy the outdoors safely and responsibly. Sophia Danenberg and other women adventurers lend support to local groups. Visit the stories, video, and photo gallery pages.

Student Conservation Association

www.thesca.org
888-722-9675; 703-524-2441
4245 North Fairfax Drive
Arlington, VA 22203

The Student Conservation Association (SCA) is America's conservation corps. Members protect and restore national parks, marine sanctuaries, cultural landmarks, and community green spaces in all 50 states. While working on projects, students can get a sense of living and working in the wilderness, like Jill Fredston did when she was a teen.

Wings WorldQuest
www.wingsworldquest.org
(646) 839-5907
17 West 17th Street, 9th Floor
New York, NY 10011
The goal of this organization, when it was first established in 1993 as Wings Trust, Inc., was to preserve the oral histories, discoveries, and accomplishments of women explorers and to help promote women working in the field sciences. In 2003, Wings WorldQuest was created to expand the mission of Wings Trust, leading to the founding of the Wings Women of Discovery Awards program, which celebrates and supports the groundbreaking work of current women explorers and scientists, including Aparajita Datta, Constanza Ceruti, Jill Fredston, Lorie Karnath, Kate Jackson, Rosaly Lopes, Meg Lowman, Stephanie Schwabe, Helen Thayer, and Edie Widder. Find out more about more about extraordinary women and extreme discoveries online.

TED Talks

"Aparajita Datta: Turning Hunters into Conservationists"
http://talentsearch.ted.com/video/Aparajita-Datta-Turning
-hunters

"Edith Widder: Glowing Life in an Underwater World"
www.ted.com/talks/edith_widder_glowing_life_in_an_under
water_world.html

"Edith Widder: The Weird, Wonderful World of Bioluminescence"
www.ted.com/talks/edith_widder_the_weird_and_wonderful
_world_of_bioluminescence.html

Other Audio and Video Links

NASA: *Through the Eyes of Scientists*: "Meet Rosaly Lopes" (video)
http://solarsystem.nasa.gov/multimedia/video-view.cfm?Vid
_ID=1047

National Geographic: *Explorers:* "Love Your Mummy" (with Constanza Ceruti; video)
http://video.nationalgeographic.com/video/specials/in-the-field
-specials/ceruti-mummy

NOVA: Profile: "Edith Widder" (video)
www.pbs.org/wgbh/nova/nature/edith-widder.html

The Planetary Society: "Fire and Ice with Volcanologist Rosaly Lopes" (audio)
www.planetary.org/multimedia/planetary-radio/show/2012/2012
0716-rosaly-lopes-volcanos.html

Wired Science: *Chat:* "Rosaly Lopes" (video)
www.tv.com/web/wired-science/watch/chat-rosaly-lopes-1863045/

Notes

Lorie Karnath: A President of Explorers

"When I first landed in Antarctica": Chronogram Magazine, April 26, 2010.
"I have five words that I think our activity": National Geographic Magazine, March 16, 2001.

PART I: CALLED BY MOUNTAINS

Annie Smith Peck: A Woman Above Them All

"Men, we all know, climb in knickerbockers": Outing, 1901.
"My allegiance previously given": Women of the Four Winds, 1985, page 11.
"My next thought was": Ibid., 1985, page 16.
"The immense glacier below": Ibid., 1985, page 33.
"A horrible nightmare": Ibid., 1985, page 55.
"$13,000 seems a large sum": A Search for the Apex of America, 1911, page 367.
"Miss Peck would make almost anyone": http://anniesmithpeck.org /2012/12/16/firsts-in-flight-the-wright-brothers-amelia-earhart -and-annie-smith-peck/.

Rosaly Lopes: Where Passion Leads

"I was always": http://volcanoworld.wordpress.com/2011/12/19/rosaly -lopes.

"In one evening, Etna taught me that": The Volcano Adventure Guide, 2005, page 217.

"He told me I couldn't understand": http://volcanoworld.wordpress .com/2011/12/19/rosaly-lopes.

"The lake appears": Ibid.

"I think that anyone": Ibid.

Constanza Ceruti: Climbing Sacred Mountains with a Humble Heart

"When I was about 14 I climbed a hill": http://sciencefriday.com/ blogs/02/04/2011/constanza-ceruti-high-altitude-archaeologist .html.

"I felt completely whole and fulfilled": Ibid.

"Few mountain climbers will": www.nationalgeographic.com/explorers /bios/constanza-ceruti.

"Just think of the Incas": Ibid.

"The boy was wearing a typical male poncho": http://sciencefriday.com /blogs/02/04/2011/constanza-ceruti-high-altitude-archaeologist .html.

"It is so humbling": www.nationalgeographic.com/explorers/bios /constanza-ceruti.

"I feel wonderful when I am in the mountains": http://sciencefriday.com /blogs/02/04/2011/constanza-ceruti-high-altitude-archaeologist .html.

"Just think of the": www.nationalgeographic.com/explorers/bios /constanza-ceruti.

Sophia Danenberg: Reaching the Highest Summit

"It's a very easy mountain": Chicago Tribune, February 1, 2008.

"He was near the top": Chicago Reader, July 13, 2006, http://www.chi-cagoreader.com/chicago/up-everest-quietly/Content?oid=922604.

"Each mountain I climbed": Flaimahmy.com, December 17, 2009, www .flaimahmy.com/2009/12/17/sophia-danenberg-on-top-of-the-world.

"A lot of people seem driven by ego": Chicago Tribune, February 1, 2008.

"I wasn't sort of thinking, 'Yeah, I'm going'": Ibid.

"Between 7 p.m. and 10 p.m. the weather": Flaimahmy.com, December 17, 2009, www.flaimahmy.com/2009/12/17/sophia-danenberg-on-top -of-the-world.

"So I was like, cool, I made it": Chicago Reader, July 13, 2006, www .chicagoreader.com/chicago/up-everest-quietly/Content?oid =922604.

"On the real Mount Everest and on the Expedition": Chicago Reader, July 13, 2006, www.chicagoreader.com/chicago/up-everest-quietly /Content?oid=922604.

PART II: SEEKING NATURE

Marianne North: Picturing Nature

"My horse was . . . very bony and old": Abundant Beauty, page 60.

"constant succession of holes": A Vision of Eden, page 163.

"He was from first to last the one idol": Ibid., page 18.

"almost impossible to leave off": Ibid., page 235.

"I am a very wild bird": The Telegraph, March 20, 2009.

In her journal she stated: A Vision of Eden, page 48.

"I had a long day's work in that lovely forest": Ibid., page 86.

"villainous-looking bandit": Ibid., page 86.

She described the forest: Ibid., page 99.

Martha Maxwell: Exploring Wildlife in the Rockies

"She would crawl though underbrush": Women in the Field, page 37.

"Clothes damp, boots hard": Martha Maxwell, Rocky Mountain Naturalist, page 81.

"We went by land and lived": Ibid., page 9.

"continual feast": Ibid., page 24.

"that soon he could claim her": Ibid., page 42.

"thick frock falling below the knee": Women in the Field, page 37.

Ynes Mexia: In Pursuit of Unknown Flora

"I found the luxuriance": Madrono, September 27, 1929, page 227.

"The collecting was very good": Women in the Field, page 107.

"I jump into boots and khaki": Sierra Club Bulletin, February 1933, page 90.

"tossed about like a straw": Ibid., page 95.

"while the smoke was annoying": Ibid., page 96.

Margaret Lowman: Life in the Treetops

"The village shaman said that if the spirits were": Life in the Treetops, page 18.

"I did not intend to climb trees": Ibid., page 15.

"My notebooks are full of numbers": News & Observer, March 30, 2012, page 2.

"My childhood aspirations had come true": Life in the Treetops, page 130.

Pamela Rasmussen: Birding Across Continents

"Pam would open the book and say": New Yorker, May 29, 2006, page 52.

"There we'd be freezing": Ibid.

"The job seemed like it was": Ibid., page 53.

"I thought to myself, if he went": Ibid., page 54.

"You can imagine the thrill": Birds of India, March 2011, www.kolkata birds.com/paminterview.htm.

Kate Jackson: In Quest of Scaly, Slimy Creatures

"It is just in my character": Harvard Magazine, March–April 2006.

"Our sensible babysitter scolded me": Mean and Lowly Things, page 90.

"He was the kind of": Ibid., page 12.

"It was a virtual blank spot": Ibid., page 14.

"Kate isn't brave, she is reckless": Telephone interview with Kate Jackson, March 17, 2012.

Aparajita Datta: Vanishing Wildlife and Forgotten People

"We are up at four ": www.nationalgeographic.com/explorers/bios /aparajita-datta.

"I finally translated my dreams of studying ecology into reality": http://ncf -india.academia.edu/AparajitaDatta.

"No time for tea": Wildlife Conservation Magazine, May–June 2005, page 1.

"*It is impossible to convince tribal*": www.nationalgeographic.com /explorers/bios/aparajita-datta.

"*The only way Namdapha can survive*": *Down to Earth*, September 15, 2005, page 49.

"*Often, an entire day's walk*": www.nationalgeographic.com/explorers /bios/aparajita-datta.

"*Don't ever lose your curiosity*": http://explore.wingsworldquest.org /aparajita_datta

PART III: EXPLORING THE WORLD'S WATERS

Eleanor Creesy: She Sets the Course

"*Her skills are considered*": www.maritimeheritage.org/ships/clippers .html.

"*The beautiful vessel*": www.sailmsc.com/Boats/club/flying_cloud.htm.

"*We have passed the Equator*": http://learningenglish.voanews.com /content/eleanor-creesy-fastest-sailing-ships-ever-built-125026174 /116534.html.

Kay Cottee: Alone on the High Seas

"*I had firmly decided on*": First Lady, page 23.
"*I started fitting it out between odd*": Ibid., page 11.
"*I looked out over the bow*": Ibid., page 43.
"*The sky was ink black*": Ibid., pages 116–117.

Edie Widder: Into the Deep, Dark Sea

"*Little dots like fairy dust, splats like puffs of liquid*": Discover Magazine, May 29, 2004.

"*Suddenly, I was*": www.pbs.org/wnet/nature/episodes/the-beauty-of -ugly/interview-dr-edith-widder/426.

"*There were explosions*": Ibid.

"*All these things are noisy*": Chronicle of Philanthropy, October 26, 2006, page 3.

"*The Navy wanted to know how*": Discover Magazine, May 29, 2004, page 3.

"*Exactly 86 seconds after we turned it on*": Chronicle of Philanthropy, October 26, 2006, page 3.

"*All of us were so amazed*": Los Angeles Times, January 8, 2013, page 1.

Jill Fredston: Rowing Along Cold Coasts

"*I just launched my boat*": Rowing to Latitude, page 4.

"*I do know, from the moment*": Ibid., page 6.

"*We became one long, gasping*": Ibid., page 10.

"*A good rowing stroke is fluid, circular*": Ibid., page 10.

"*The river speaks a language rich in verbs*": Ibid., page 104.

Stephanie Schwabe: Diving into the Dark Frontier

"*You feel like the clutter of the surface*": Geotimes, July 2008, page 1.

"*Could a person with the life-long*": Living in Darkness, page 16.

"*In that short period of time*": Ibid., page 16.

"*It was like my spirit had*": Ibid., page 102.

"*I saw recently that*": Herald-Leader, March 15, 2011.

PART IV: LONG TREKS

Isabella Bird Bishop: Health, Horses, Adventure

"*My pack, with my*": A Lady's Life in the Rocky Mountains, page 56.

"*the mightiest volcano*": Victorian Lady Travellers, page 23.

"*leaping from rock to rock*": A Lady's Life in the Rocky Mountains, page 107

"*He is a man any woman*": Victorian Lady Travellers, page 34.

"*the appetite of a tiger*": Ibid., page 39.

"*hard, hungry, silver-grey Arab*": Ibid., page 41.

"*shrieking, yelling, and juggling*": Ibid., page 48.

"*evil glare in his eyes*": Ibid., page 48.

Annie Kopchovsky "Londonderry": Pedaling Around the World with Chutzpah

"*I stand and rejoice every time*": Around the World on Two Wheels, page 142.

"*I didn't want to spend my life at*": Ibid., page 12.

"sailed away like a kite": The Christian Science Monitor, August 28, 2009.
"Although I've cheek enough to go": Around the World on Two Wheels, page 42.
"a '30 mile spin' around the city": Ibid., page 71.

Helga Estby: The Long Walk Across America

"We were told at the start we would never": Bold Spirit, page 99.
"given both herself and her daughter": Ibid., page 107.
"They had been lost in forests": Ibid., page 129.

Freya Stark: A Fashionable Nomad

this initial *"moment of emancipation"*: A Passionate Nomad: The Life of Freya Stark, page 22.
"This is the great moment": Valley of the Assassins, page 170.
"The greatest and almost": A Passionate Nomad: The Life of Freya Stark, page 106.

Alexandra David-Néel: Seeking the Unknown

"I craved to go beyond the": My Journey to Lhasa, page xvii.
awed by the *"calm solitudes"*: My Journey to Lhasa, page xxxiii.
"Any honest traveler": Ibid., page xxxix.
"People whose hearts are not": Ibid., page 32.
"The majestic Kha Karpo towering": Ibid., page 3.
"Now we could discern the elegant": Ibid., page 255.

Helen Thayer: Facing Fear in the Far North

"One part of me wanted to go": Polar Dream, page 34.
"They told me": Historylink.org, August 12, 2011, www.historylink.org/index.cfm?DisplayPage=output.cfm&file_id=9848.
"The Arctic has rammed everything down my throat": Polar Dream, page 208.
"I want them to say": HistoryLink.org, August 12, 2011, www.historylink.org/index.cfm?DisplayPage=output.cfm&file_id=9848.

Kira Salak: Discoveries in Two Worlds

"I always needed to be gone": Four Corners, page 10.

"Traveling could allow me": Ibid., page 17.

"The jungle unfolds us in its tangled": Ibid., page 247.

"a real life Lara Croft": www.nationalgeographic.com/explorers/bios/kira-salak.

"it had become a 'fickle parent'": The Cruelest Journey, page 91.

"When they say I can't": www.nationalgeographic.com/explorers/bios/kira-salak.

Bibliography

BOOKS

Benson, Maxine. *Women in the West: Martha Maxwell, Rocky Mountain Naturalist*. Lincoln: University of Nebraska Press, 1986.

Bird, Isabella L. *A Lady's Life in the Rocky Mountains*. Norman: University of Oklahoma Press, 1977.

———. *Unbeaten Tracks in Japan*, reprint of 1880 edition. Rutland, VT, C. E. Tuttle Company, 1973.

Bonta, Marcia Meyers. *Women in the Field: America's Pioneering Women Naturalists*. College Station, TX: Texas A&M University Press, 1991.

Cottee, Kay. *First Lady*. Sydney, Australia: Pan Australia, 1990.

David-Néel, Alexandra. *My Journey to Lhasa*. Boston: Beacon Books, 1993.

Foster, Barbara and Michael Foster. *The Secret Lives of Alexandra David-Neel*. 1st edition. Woodstock, NY: Overlook Press, 1998.

Fredston, Jill. *Rowing to Latitude: Journeys Along the Arctic's Edge*. New York: North Point Press, 2001.

———. *Snowstruck: In the Grip of Avalanches*. New York: Harcourt, 2005.

Geniesse, Jane Fletcher. *A Passionate Nomad: The Life of Freya Stark*. New York: Random House, 1999.

Hunt, Linda Lawrence. *Bold Spirit: Helga Estby's Forgotten Walk Across Victorian America*. New York: Anchor Books, 2003.

Jackson, Kate. *Mean and Lowly Things: Snakes, Science, and Survival in the Congo*. Cambridge, MA: Harvard University Press, 2008.

Lopes, Rosaly. *The Volcano Adventure Guide*. Cambridge, United Kingdom: Cambridge University Press, 2005.

———. *Volcanoes*. Oxford, Great Britain: One World Publications, 2010.

Lopes, Rosaly M. C. and Tracy K. P. Gregg. *Volcanic Worlds*. Chichester, Great Britain: Praxis Publishing, 2004

Lowman, Margaret D. *Life in the Treetops, Adventures of a Woman in Field Biology*. New Haven, CT: Yale University Press, 1999.

Middleton, Dorothy. *Victorian Lady Travellers*. New York: E.P. Dutton, 1965.

North, Marianne. *A Vision of Eden*. Exeter, United Kingdom: Webb and Bower Publishers, 1980.

———. *Abundant Beauty*. Vancouver, Canada: Greystone Books, D&M Publishers, 2010.

Olds, Elizabeth Fagg. *Women of the Four Winds: The Adventures of Four of America's First Women Explorers*. Boston: Houghton Mifflin, 1985.

Peck, Annie Smith. *A Search for the Apex of America: High Mountain Climbing in Peru and Bolivia, Including the Conquest of Huascarán, with Some Observations on the Country and People Below*. New York: Dodd, Mead, 1911.

Salak, Kira. *Four Corners: A Journey into the Heart of Papua New Guinea*. Washington, DC: Counterpoint, 2001.

———. *The Cruelest Journey: 600 Miles to Timbuktu*. Washington, DC: National Geographic, 2005.

———. *The White Mary*. New York: Henry Holt, 2008.

Schoonover, Jason. *Adventurous Dreams, Adventurous Lives*. Surrey, British Columbia: Rocky Mountain Books, 2007.

Schwabe, Stephanie Jutta. *Living in Darkness*. Huntsville, AL: National Speleological Society, 2009.

Shaw, David W. *Flying Cloud: The True Story of America's Most Famous Clipper Ship and the Woman Who Guided Her*. New York: William Morrow, 2000.

Stark, Freya. *Valley of the Assassins and other Persian Travels*. London: John Murray, 1934.

Thayer, Helen. *Polar Dream: The First Solo Expedition by a Woman and Her Dog to the Magnetic North Pole*. New York: Simon and Schuster, 1993.

Zheutlin, Peter. *Around the World on Two Wheels: Annie Londonderry's Extraordinary Ride*. New York: Citadel Press Books, 2007.

INTERVIEWS

Telephone Interview with Lori Karnath, February 2, 2012.

Telephone Interview with Rosaly Lopes, February 7, 2012.

Telephone Interview with Kate Jackson, March 17, 2012.

E-mail Interview with Constanza Ceruti, April 25, 2012.

Telephone Interview with Margaret Lowman, May 20, 2012.

Telephone Interview with Kira Salak, July 26, 2012.

Telephone Interview with Pamela Rasmussen, August 30, 2012.

Telephone interview with Jill Fredston, October 4, 2012.

Telephone Interview with Edie Widder, October 11, 2012.

Telephone Interview with Stephanie Jutta Schwabe, November 26, 2012.

E-mail Interview with Aparajita Datta, November 28, 2012.

JOURNALS

Datta, A., J. Pansa, M.D. Madhusudan, and C. Mishra. "Discovery of the Leaf Deer (*Muntiacus ptaoensis*) in Arunachal Pradesh: An Addition to the Large Mammals of India." *Current Science* 84 (2003): 454–458.

Jackson, Kate, and David C. Blackburn. "The Amphibians and Reptiles of Nouabale-Ndoki National Park, Republic of Congo (Brazzaville)." *Salamandra* 43 no. 3 (August 20, 2007): 149–164.

Mexia, Ynes. "Botanical Trails in Old Mexico," *Madrono* 1 (September 27, 1929): 227–240.

———. "Three Thousand Miles Up the Amazon." *Sierra Club Bulletin* (February 1933): 88–96.

Previgliano, C.H., C. Ceruti, J. Reinhard, F.A. Araoz, and J. G. Diez. "Radiologic Evaluation of the Llullaillaco Mummies." *American Journal of Roentgenology* 181 (2003): 1473–1479.

Rasmussen, Pamela C. "Apparent Sibling Cannibalism by a Nestling Pigeon Guillemot." *The Wilson Bulletin* 100, no. 1 (March 1988).

———. "Relationships Between Coastal South American King and Blue-Eyed Shags." *The Condor* 93, no. 4 (November 1991): 825–839.

Rasmussen, Pamela C., and Farah Ishtiaq. "Vocalizations and Behaviour of the Forest Owlet." *Forktail Journal of Asian Ornithology* 15 (August 1999): 61–65.

Rasmussen, Pamela C., Thein Aung, and John H. Rappole. "Breeding Avifauna of the Sub-Himalayan Zone of Northern Kachin State, Myanmar." *Ornithological Monographs* 70, no. 1 (February 15, 2011): 95–108.

MAGAZINES

Brown, Nell Porter. "Nothing to Fear: Travels with a Snake Lover." *Harvard Magazine*, March–April 2006.

Datta, Aparajita." "High on Hornbills." *Wildlife Conservation Magazine*, May–June 2005.

———. Fading Fauna, Forgotten People." *Down to Earth*, September 15, 2005.

Falke, Stefan. "The Ambassador." *Outside Magazine*, June 17, 2011.

Felshman, Jeffrey. "Up Everest, Quietly: Sophia Danenberg Was the First Black Woman to Sit on Top of the World and Nobody Noticed." *Chicago Reader*, July 13, 2006, http://www.chicagoreader.com/chicago/up-everest-quietly/Content?oid=922604.

McClintock, Jack. "Splendor in the Dark." *Discover Magazine*, May 29, 2004.

Michaels, Marty. "Turning Back the Tide." *Chronicle of Philanthropy*, October 26, 2006.

Milius, S. "Glow-in-the-Dark Shark Has Killer Smudge." *Science News*, August 1, 1998.

———. "Octopus Suckers Glow in Deep, Dark Sea." *Science News*, March 13, 1999.

Ordansky, Jesse. "Local Luminary: Lorie Karnath." *Chronogram Magazine*, April 26, 2010.

Reinhard, Johan, and Maria Stenzel. "At 22,000 Feet Children of Inca Sacrifice Found Frozen in Time." *National Geographic*, November 1999.

Schwabe, Stephanie Jutta. "Floor of Fire." *Divernet Magazine*, January 2004.

Seabrook, John. "Ruffled Feathers." *New Yorker*, May 29, 2006.

Snedden, Megan "Former Explorers Club President Talks Travel." *National Geographic*, April 5, 2012.

Tachibana, Chris. "Congo Calling." *The Scientist*, October 1, 2010.

Wayman, Erin. "Down to Earth with Stephanie Schwabe." *Geotimes*, July 2008.

NEWSPAPERS

Burt, Sheila."Mountain Climber Has Soared High Since Homewood Days: Sophia Danenberg the 1st African-American to Reach Mt. Everest Summit." *Chicago Tribune*. February 1, 2008.

Flint, Peter, "Dame Freya Stark, Travel Writer, Is Dead at 100." *New York Times*. May 11, 1993.

Hughes, Kathryn. "Marianne North: The Flower Huntress." *The Telegraph*. March 20, 2009.

Menconi, David. "Scientist Margaret Lowman's Profile Rises as Head of the New N.C. Nature Research Center."*News Observer*. April 1, 2012.

Netburn, Deborah. "Elusive Giant Squid Caught on Video for the First Time." *Los Angeles Times*. January 8, 2013.

Warren, Jim. "Scientist Wants to Get Back to Her Lab: Underwater Caves." *Herald-Leader*. March 15, 2011.

Zheutlin, Peter. "Backstory: Chasing Annie Londonderry." *The Christian Science Monitor*. August 28, 2009.

ONLINE FORUMS AND BLOGS

Bartlett, Thomas. "Dr. Stephanie Schwabe." Online Forum, Chum Social Dive Club: Houston, TX. www.chumclub.org/forums /showthread.php?171-Dr-Stephanie-Schwabe.

Polk, Milbry. "Constanza Ceruti, High Altitude Archeologist." *Science Friday* blog. February 4, 2011. http://sciencefriday.com/blogs /02/04/2011/constanza-ceruti-high-altitude-archaeologist.html.

Potts, Mary Ann. "The Future of Exploration: An Interview with Explorers Club President Lorie Karnath." *Beyond the Edge*. National Geographic Society blog. March 16, 2001. http://adventureblog .nationalgeographic.com/tag/lorie-karnath.

WEBSITES

Annie Smith Peck: A Woman's Place Is at the Top. "Peck's Bio." http:// anniesmithpeck.org/pecks-bio-4.
BlackPast.org. "Danenberg, Sophia (1972–)." www.blackpast.org/?q =aah/danenberg-sophia-1972.
Ember, Steve, and Shirley Griffith. "The Woman Who Guided the Flying Cloud." Explorations in VOA Special English. Last updated July 5, 2011. http://learningenglish.voanews.com/content/eleanor -creesy-fastest-sailing-ships-ever-built-125026174/116534.html.
Felshman, Jeffrey. "Up Everest, Quietly: Sophia Danenberg Was the First Black Woman to Sit on Top of the World and Nobody Noticed." *Chicago Reader*. July 13, 2006. http://www.chicagoreader. com/chicago/up-everest-quietly/Content?oid=922604.
Flaimahmy.com. "Sophia Danenberg: On Top of the World." December 17, 2009. www.flaimahmy.com/2009/12/17/sophia-danenberg -on-top-of-the-world.
Grewal, Bikram. "Pamela C. Rasmussen: A Birds of India Interview." May 2011. www.kolkatabirds.com/paminterview.htm.
Kershner, Kate. "Thayer, Helen (b. 1937), Sportswoman, Explorer, Essay 9848." HistoryLink.org. August 12, 2011. www.historylink .org/index.cfm?DisplayPage=output.cfm&file_id=9848.
Mills, James. "Wired—Exploring The Adventure Gap." *Alpinist*. January 2, 2012. www.alpinist.com/doc/ALP40/40-wired.
National Geographic Society. *Emerging Explorers*: "Constanza Ceruti: Anthropologist/Archaeologist." www.nationalgeographic.com /explorers/bios/constanza-ceruti/.
National Geographic Society. *Emerging Explorers*: "Kira Salak: Writer/ Adventurer." www.nationalgeographic.com/explorers/bios/kira -salak.

National Oceanic and Atmospheric Administration. *Ocean Explorer*: "Edith A. Widder: OceanAGE Career Profile." http://ocean explorer.noaa.gov/edu/oceanage/04widder.

Nature Conservation Foundation. "Aparajita Datta." http://ncf-india .academia.edu/AparajitaDatta.

PBS. *Nature*: "The Beauty of Ugly: Interview: Dr. Edith Widder." www .pbs.org/wnet/nature/episodes/the-beauty-of-ugly/interview -dr-edith-widder/426.

Peckyno, Robert. "Interview: Rosaly M.C. Lopes, Planetary Scientist." Volcano World. Oregon State University Department of Geosciences. December 19, 2011. http://volcano.oregonstate.edu /rosaly-lopes.

Potter, Dr. Russell A. "Annie Smith Peck 1850–1935: Scholar and Mountaineer." www.ric.edu/faculty/rpotter/smithpeck.html.

TED Conferences, Inc. "Constanza Ceruti: High-Altitude Archaeologist + Anthropologist." TED Fellow Network. http://fellows.ted .com/profiles/constanza-ceruti.

The Clipper Flying Cloud. www.sailmsc.com/Boats/club/flying _cloud.htm.

The Maritime Heritage Project. maritimeheritage.org/captains/ creesy.html.

Index